D0820006

THRIVING IN THE NEW ECONOMY

Lessons from Today's Top Business Minds

LORI ANN LAROCCO

John Wiley & Sons, Inc.

Published by John Wiley & Sons, Inc., Hoboken, New Jersey.
Published simultaneously in Canada.

For general information on our other products and services or for technical support, please contact our Customer Care Department within the United States at (800) 762-2974, outside the United States at (317) 572-3993 or fax (317) 572-4002.

Wiley also publishes its books in a variety of electronic formats. Some content that appears in print may not be available in electronic books. For more information about Wiley products, visit our web site at www.wiley.com.

ISBN: 978-0-470-55731-0

Printed in the United States of America

10 9 8 7 6 5 4 3 2 1

This book is dedicated to my true companion—
my husband, Michael—
and my three wonderful children:
Nicholas, Declan, and Abigail.
Thank you for understanding mommy's even crazier schedule.

Contents

FOREWORD

H. Wayne Huizenga

Today we find ourselves in what may be the most troubled economy in three generations. For a good number of Americans, the biggest concern isn't how to survive in today's new economy—it's how to thrive in it. There were signs. All of us could see that we were due for a rough patch.

What no one could have predicted with any confidence was just how rough that patch would be. After all, you have government doing what it can to overstep its bounds. Every day, Washington is making decisions it simply has no business making, deciding which companies continue and which ones fold up.

That's not capitalism, and it's certainly not a free market. There are plenty of companies out there that are successful even in today's downturn, and they deserve the exact same opportunity to succeed that their predecessors did. In fact, when you consider that these companies are prospering in the face of such extraordinarily dire circumstances, you could credibly argue that they deserve even greater latitude to conduct their affairs in the manner of their choosing. After all, they're the ultimate survivors, the companies most able to prove their value to the marketplace at a time when the marketplace is most resistant.

These are businesses whose leaders have a genuinely rare combination of vision, ingenuity, and energy. People whose fortunes rise and fall based on the decisions they make every day—and who excel at making great decisions time and again.

Compare them with the government bureaucrats making their own decisions about the businesses they run. These are people who frequently have little or no corporate experience, who've seldom had to worry about whether the choices they make today will benefit them directly or influence the prospects of the organization they work for. Yet these are the people making rules that impact the world of business arbitrarily and capriciously.

That isn't to say that I believe business is without blame in our current environment. Too many companies have indeed stepped over the line. And yes, we do need some realignment to address these excesses. But we must temper that with the understanding that the more regulated we become, the less free we become.

In fact, I believe with everything I am that maintaining free markets is the single most effective thing we can do to foster continued growth and opportunity in the United States. There is no such thing as a limit on the number of visionaries out there. A new Bill Gates could be in the making right now. There's a good chance the next Warren Buffett is entering business school in the fall semester. And there are certainly others with the talent and drive to eclipse my own accomplishments. Their fields may be varied—for some of them, their fields may not even exist yet—but the one thing they all need collectively to succeed is a fair and functioning free market system.

I look at Mike Jackson of AutoNation, Mike Duke of Walmart, Evan Williams of Twitter, and Wilbur Ross of WL Ross & Co.; all of them are people who are leading, changing the market, and yes, making money in an environment like this. Although each has a different story to tell, they all share the leadership and foresight that allowed them to take advantage of a changing economy and reach out to consumers with a proposition that proved compelling, even in challenging times.

This book looks at how real leaders tackle crisis and succeed—how they take a risk, plan for the future, and create growth opportunities. It's about how real leaders managed to thrive in our new economy. Spend time with its subjects, and you'll see that opportunity does indeed exist and that the best role for government to play is as a partner to enterprise, helping promote an environment that rewards innovation, diligence, and creativity.

Ultimately, I believe that organically successful companies—that is, companies that generate their own success by interacting favorably with the market—will prove themselves to be today's truest winners. When the economy inevitably recovers, they will be the ones to emerge with the strongest brands in their fields and the greatest prospects for ongoing growth. But for this to happen, and for our economy as a whole to become healthy again, we must follow the free market model. Flawed as it may be, it still undeniably provides the world's greatest opportunity for business to thrive.

H. Wayne Huizenga is one of America's greatest entrepreneurs. He founded Blockbuster and AutoNation and is owner of the Miami Dolphins.

PREFACE

History's defining moments have taught us that leaders are tested, made, or broken, and we are living in one of those moments right now. When the markets collapsed in September 2008—and as one spectacular failure rode on the heels of another—people wondered when it would end. As we entered each weekend of that month, my CNBC show *Squawk Box* left the guest list loose. There was no sense in trying to fill up the show with guests for Monday when we had two entire days left between shows, and *anything* could happen. The weekends quickly turned into a "wait and see" of which company would fail and which one Uncle Sam would rescue. We would book our Monday morning news makers on Sunday.

This market crisis took me back to my years as the night side assignment editor at WFTV-TV in Orlando. The wildfires of the 1990s were consuming hundreds of acres in central Florida; the winds were picking up, and there was no rain in sight to quench the parched soil. Despite the fact that the flames were miles away, I can remember the dense, stifling smell of the forest fires hanging in the newsroom. Watching the images of flames several stories high swallowing up trees and homes in a blink, I thought to myself, *When will this end?* No one knew; we were in unchartered territory. A crisis like this had no timeline. The unknown was the most frightening thing we were facing.

The September 2008 economic crisis was in fact a firestorm engulfing the markets. Much like the massive Florida wildfires of the 1990s, we were reporting on events we had never seen before. We were reporting on history. No one knew when the market turmoil would end or what kind of reaction the rest of the world would have to the U.S. markets. It was a global crisis. Both Main Street and Wall Street depended on our program for unbiased, actionable, and up-to-the-minute information. It's a responsibility we never took lightly.

The mantra "too big to fail" became the "it" phrase as investors tried to wrap their arms around what was happening. The 401(k) plan quickly became "201k," and the once-golden boys of Wall Street joined thousands of others who were out of jobs. But despite the credit crunch and economic headwinds, there are captains of industry out there who are not only surviving but thriving in this the "New Economy," and what makes these leaders unique are the strategies they employ. They are the ultimate chess players in the economy game. By offering advice, cutting budgets by millions of dollars, and meticulously managing their investments, these pace-setters are navigating through the turbulent markets—and not being swallowed up in the undertow. As Senior Talent Producer for CNBC, I am lucky to speak with some of the world's richest and most successful businesspeople on a daily basis.

To write this book, I opened my "trillion dollar" Rolodex—as others in my industry call it—because it contains a trillion-dollar money manager, a baker's dozen of billionaires, and countless millionaires—and sat down with some of my close contacts. Here, I have asked them not only to explain how they are responding to these historic times, but more importantly, how they have been able to defy failure and what opportunities they currently see. Although their industries and backgrounds may be different, they all share the same qualities that enable them to be leaders. They are nimble, forward-looking, and opportunistic, and all refuse to have a challenge take them down. These individuals are thriving in the new economy.

Part One

The Economy

1

Larry Lindsey

No matter what state the markets are in, there are a handful of economic and strategist "go-to" people I always rely on. Larry Lindsey, CEO of the economic advisory firm The Lindsey Group, is one of them. What makes Larry stand out from the hundreds of other economists out there is that he not only cares about the topics he discusses but can break them down in such a way that makes them understandable and interesting to those watching and listening (which, believe it or not, is hard to do when it comes to a television interview). We want the guests on my show to offer our viewers actionable information. Lengthy discourse, although occasionally colorful, is not all that useful; and Larry gets that. I have known Larry for years. I've found him to be always candid, and his global economic contacts are some of the best.

(*continued*)

(*continued*)

Before his latest private venture, Larry was a man of the beltway. He served as director of the National Economic Council from 2001 to 2002, and was the assistant to the president on economic policy for U.S. President George W. Bush. In fact, Larry was one of the leaders crafting President Bush's $1.35 trillion tax cut plan, calling it an "insurance policy" against an economic downturn. Back in 1996—while acting as a governor of the Federal Reserve Board—Lindsey made headlines for spotting the appearance of the late 1990s U.S. stock market bubble.

Today, as CEO of The Lindsey Group, Larry examines global macroeconomic trends and events that can significantly influence his firm's financial markets and economic performance. Larry breaks down today's navigation of the economic crisis into a formula of three different qualities of leadership that one must have to thrive in the new economy and details how he uses them to grow his company and counsel clients.

Three decades serving in a variety of positions in government, academia, and the private sector have convinced me that one of our society's greatest weaknesses, when dealing with crises, is that managerial and rhetorical leadership qualities have crowded out simple analytics. The reason for this is the confusion that exists between leadership and followership. Most institutions prefer managers who will serve the needs of an existing institution—that is, who will follow the wishes of the various constituencies within the institution—rather than managers who will lead the institution to a new place.

Our political process is dominated by leaders who tell us what they think we want to hear, thereby effectively following the polls and the media and not necessarily leading the country. Worse, our government has created institutional barriers around our leaders that actually prevent them from hearing a variety of analytic points of view in the name of minimizing the influence of "special interests." Similarly, they discourage those who have actually been analytically successful outside of government from entering public service by the current vetting process. For example, the usual connotation of leadership is wrapped up in the presence of followers. After all, one can hardly call oneself a "leader" if no one is following behind. This is true of the lieutenant who inspires the troops into battle and is also the case for a political leader who, after all, doesn't *become* a leader unless he or she has more followers than the opponent on Election Day. But that type of leadership by itself can actually be a handicap for a society dealing with a financial or economic catastrophe. To be precise, financial crises throughout history have developed when excesses went unchecked. Like the over-leveraging of risk in our capital system. All these manias, panics, and bubbles have the same characteristic: the absence of real leadership that takes a contrarian perspective. None of this is a criticism of the actions of political and financial leaders in this or any other crisis; the problem seems to be structural. Societies create institutions that have built-in biases and constraints, and these leaders have very little choice but to carry out the institutional imperative. Indeed, that is their job as leaders of institutions.

One of the most unfortunate examples of this flawed model of leadership was a comment made by Citigroup CEO Chuck Prince in July 2007, when he said of the bank he was supposedly leading: "As long as the music plays, you've got to get up and dance. We're still dancing." This quote shows that despite his personal skepticism about the ability of the market to continue with its excesses, the institutional demands of his firm required him, as a leader, to override his personal cautionary views—and forced his firm to continue on with the practices that ultimately led to disaster in the first place.

In fact, as much as we and they like to deny it now, both politicians and market participants actually *demanded* that firms continued to "dance"—and that the band keep playing during the run up to the current crisis. Leverage was encouraged—not discouraged—by market players, including most notably many self-described "shareholder activists," who acted in the name of creating "shareholder value." The markets rewarded earnings growth and ruthlessly punished firms that balanced the pursuit of profit with a healthy respect for risk. Members of both political parties pushed for ever-higher degrees of homeownership and demanded that lenders and mortgage securitizers give ever-increasing amounts of loans to less qualified borrowers. Leaders who did not dance to this tune faced condemnation in the press, challenges to their positions by irate shareholders, and withering criticism from members of Congress.

The First Economic Avalanche

It was clear that it was all going to come crashing down; the question was how. Usually such crashes happen like avalanches; a small change somewhere in the structure finds a critical point of weakness. Relationships and transactions that had held together no longer do. Finally—and what appears on the surface to be suddenly—the whole hill collapses.

The initial weakness here was housing. While serving on the Federal Reserve Board, I was the governor responsible for housing and community affairs issues back in the 1990s during the last housing recession—and it taught me a lot about mortgage markets. We had warned clients—and as the *New York Times* reported, the White House—in late 2005 that a housing bubble was forming and that action should be taken to prevent consequent problems. Housing had not had a catastrophic nationwide collapse since the 1930s; it was generally viewed as an impossibility. By the middle of 2007, there had been a slight deterioration in housing prices, with the Case Shiller index down 5 percent. Housing inventories appeared to have stabilized, and a wide variety of commentators and government officials had concluded that the housing recession had bottomed.

At that point we concluded that far from ending, the avalanche was only about to begin unless something was done. The key was to stop or sharply slow the pace of subprime lending. These mortgages constituted 24 percent of the total dollar volume of mortgages in 2006, an unsustainable number. Some of the mortgage market reforms we had instituted in the 1990s to encourage homeownership had helped create the subprime market. But around the time I left the Fed, it was tightly controlled and constituted only about 3 percent of all mortgages. As the late Herb Stein used to say, "When a trend is unsustainable, it will stop." But this particular trend was the self-perpetuating kind. If subprime mortgages stopped being granted, demand for houses would collapse; this, in turn, would mean fewer buyers and lower prices throughout the market. In July 2007, we estimated that the pace of home sales would drop by at least another 1.5 million—more than twice the drop that had occurred so far. While others were predicting that the bottom had been reached, we saw that there was still a substantial downside risk that the weight of inventories would cause prices to crack and that a self-reinforcing cycle where foreclosures and prices start to interact more directly would begin.

Later that month, while market indices reached double what they had been for the previous four and a half years and were still on their way to a new high, we identified for our clients the likely place where the avalanche would begin. We wrote that "the biggest risk lies with the intermediaries in the leverage game—the big players in the financial arena—whose top line is driven by fee income from doing the deals and whose balance sheets are crammed full of inventory waiting to be dumped on some buyer." We identified the market's faulty logic as this: "If something goes wrong with the financial system, the world's central banks will have no choice but to open the liquidity spigots and play lender of last resort. Heads you win, tails the system gets bailed out taking you along with it."

That was 14 months before Lehman Brothers' collapse. The problem with the logic up to that point, as we identified it, was that "the relative prices of assets and goods can only vary so far." Given their pace of divergence, we questioned, "Will these momentums play on asset prices and continue for another year? Probably. Eighteen months? Possibly. Two years? Probably not. Enjoy the party, but also be ready to leave when the hosts start looking worried." The reason for the timing was the parabolic rate at which asset prices were climbing. The music probably had to stop playing for these intermediaries before the end of 2008—and certainly before the middle of 2009.

The Best Offense Is a Good Defense

There is only one way to deal with an impending avalanche: get out of the way! Although our clients' base is quite diverse, whatever their responsibilities, the key for them was to assume a defensive posture. This became clearer as—following the avalanche analogy—other cracks were starting to appear in the financial structure, particularly in the area of consumer finance. In March 2008, I appeared on the show *Squawk Box,* which Lori Ann LaRocco produces for CNBC, with former Treasury Secretary John Snow. I warned that auto finance was the next shoe to drop, and jokingly added that by the end of the year, people would have to go to their local Federal Reserve Bank to get an auto loan. As it turned out, the auto finance companies were the ones going to the Fed; it was still providing the money.

At this point, the financial system was doing its best to paper over the cracks in the ice sheet. On July 14 we noted that although Freddie Mac had reported that it had $16 billion in stockholder's equity in a supplement to their GAAP (Generally Accepted Accounting Principle) numbers, the firm had also reported that they had a net asset value of negative $5 billion under Fair Value Accounting. We noted that a similar exposure existed at Fannie Mae and that the amount of leverage both companies had to home prices meant that things could deteriorate very quickly. Both stocks rallied that week on the seeming "good news" in their quarterly report. However, it was to be short lived.

Two months later, Lehman Brothers collapsed, and a panicked Washington rushed to fill the breech. We wrote to our clients, "For all the observations by policy makers that the market had six months to prepare for Lehman, [these] policy makers themselves had not been fully prepared for this further deterioration in markets. During this time, many of the activities in Washington were designed for publicity but had little developed policy behind it." The shocker about Lehman Brothers—and particularly, the rescue of AIG—was that policy makers were essentially making up the rules as they went along. That point was crucial. In the same note to clients, we predicted that the Troubled Asset Relief Program (TARP) designed to purchase distressed assets in an attempt to fortify the financial sector would not work; and indeed, after many false starts, it didn't.

Our focus shifted from the inevitable market meltdown to the government's efforts to repair the damage. In a piece on March 11, we laid out the details of what was likely to work and what was not likely to work. This remains very much a work in progress and is the center of our attention and the attention of my company.

Thriving Criteria

To put it mildly, we are an unusual firm. I doubt very much that my high school guidance counselor had anything like my current job in his great catalog of "things you can do when you grow up." We believe that analytic leadership is in short supply and that it is our job to provide it. But given the shortage of road maps in this regard, we have had to make up our own guideposts and have settled on three: independence, objectivity, and candor. Although these are great words, implementing them can be challenging—because none of them represents a path to popularity.

Independence requires we not be tied to any existing institution. Chuck Prince's private analysis—and given the e-mail trails that are now being revealed, probably those of many other corporate leaders—was that the financial system was on an unsustainable path. But the needs of the institutions they led demanded that they stay on it. Moreover, a variety of in-house analytic shops in the financial sector had encountered some difficulty in recent years as their forecasts became suspect. Markets wondered whether these in-house shops could keep their independence or whether the interest of the institution that was paying their salaries would influence their decision. Even if the individuals involved did their best to preserve their autonomy, they would still face market skepticism. So we concluded that the only way to preserve independence is to actually *be* independent. We are unaffiliated with any organization, and we make sure that our cash flow is not dependent on any single client.

Ahead of the Crisis

We were very early in warning about the likelihood of a housing market crash. We had begun to caution our clients in late 2005 about potential trouble ahead. One of our clients, a national firm, had significant exposure to that segment of the economy. Our analysis was hotly debated within the firm because, if we were right, it would require a significant change in their corporate strategy to prepare for the tough times ahead. The firm lightened up on debt financing and expansion plans, which, at the time, was an extremely unpopular decision in the markets. With leverage and expansion held down, profit growth stagnated; and with it, so did the share price. This was in the midst of a rising stock market and ever-increasing leverage. The decision contributed to calls for the resignation of the CEO. Housing inventory began to stabilize in the middle of 2006, and the consensus was that the "housing cycle had bottomed." This implied that the CEO had made the wrong call, which was a contributing factor in his departure.

Although some believed housing had bottomed at that point, we continued conveying to our clients a decidedly downbeat long-term housing and economic forecast. In mid-2007, we warned them that "a collapse of subprime lending back to its historical pace could take $1.5 million off annual home sales in the aggregate." Worse, we extended our forecast for the housing downturn, writing that "our assumption has been that 2008 would be the bottom of the housing market. But it is not clear how the inventory overhang will correct itself by then." We went on to warn that "there is still a substantial downside risk that the weight of inventories will finally cause home prices to crack." At that time, the Case Shiller index had house prices down only 5 percent, while most forecasts were indicating that housing had bottomed.

Fortunately, the new CEO of the client firm was convinced by our analysis, and the firm continued to reduce its exposure to a still-potential and prospective housing decline. In retrospect, it was our independence that had been crucial to this outcome. Had we been physically housed in corporate headquarters or had we been members of the board, our ability to be self-regulating would have been compromised. At a minimum, we would likely have been perceived as taking sides in office politics, with the possibility that our own position within the firm would have been jeopardized. Indeed, it was our independence that most likely provided the credibility to our forecast that tipped the scales within the firm.

The Next Shoe to Drop

Another quality needed to thrive in times of crisis is objectivity. Although sometimes confused with independence, this attribute is actually far harder to achieve. Whereas, independence is a physical trait—at least on an organizational chart—objectivity is a state of mind. It requires that you do not get caught up in the moment. And even the best of us is influenced by what is happening around us. Momentum trading is an extreme view of this, which implicitly assumes that Newton's law that "an object in motion will stay in motion" applies here as well, at least until some outside force affects it. Moreover, we all have a tendency to talk our book—and an even deeper psychological need to be right. This tends to keep us in our positions longer than we should be. On the other hand, there is also an inclination to overcompensate for this, which turns us into nervous Nellies and changes our view with each piece of data that happens to go the other way.

Objectivity requires perspective. It requires knowing what data are important and what are not and knowing when there is a critical mass of contrary evidence to force one to change one's view. By far, the most useful tools in acquiring a perspective is a knowledge and sense of history. History, by definition, takes you out of the moment. By far the biggest trap that caused many to lose objectivity in the months leading up to the current crisis was the widespread view in the economics profession and in financial markets that we were in the midst of a "Great Moderation."* However, the Great Moderation was actually a historical moment lasting 25 years, not a permanent development.

As we saw the crisis unfolding in June 2007, we sent our clients a message titled "The Next Shoe to Drop: Credit Spreads." We noted that too much confidence can depress returns to risk and lead to capital being diverted into projects that will, on average, lose money. Financial assets had risen in value, which raised wealth-to-income ratios and therefore consumption-to-income ratios, thereby depressing new savings. We predicted that spreads would rise and that ironically, this would take a good deal of pressure off the yield curve in the riskless market, leading to a rally in government bonds and a lower Fed funds rate. On September 12, we predicted that the Fed would begin a series of rate cuts at their Tuesday meeting, with an initial 50 basis point cut, but noted that even this cut would be unlikely to unfreeze credit markets; we

Author's note: The "Great Moderation" is a phrase used to describe the post-Reagan period from roughly 1981 to 2007, during which interest rates and credit spreads dropped and equity premiums rose sharply.

further predicted a series of cuts in Fed funds to at least 3.5 percent. More than 90 percent of analysts surveyed had predicted just a 25 basis point cut. At its October meeting, the Fed cut only a quarter point and declared the risks to be "balanced." We warned our clients that although this might be the case, the risks had not gone away—and that the Federal Open Market Committee (FOMC) would soon change its views.

Law of Unintended Consequences

One of history's great lessons is that policy makers, in both the public and private sectors, tend to underestimate the costs involved when they contemplate the actions necessary to address some adverse change in circumstances. Although this is due in part to long periods of conditioning to the relationships and magnitudes that existed before the crisis, an equally important cause of the underestimation is the Law of Unintended Consequences. Even the most carefully designed policy responses involve unforeseen results, and in a crisis, there is not the time for as careful a consideration of the consequences of policy as might be ideal.

Risks in Believing in Solely on History

However, just as knowledge of history provides a tremendous advantage in trying to be objective, there are huge risks in believing too literally that history repeats itself. This is most apparent today in a widespread view that we are in for another Great Depression. Our company has never been in that camp. Our forecast at the end of 2007 called for a peak unemployment rate of about 10.5 percent before it would begin to decline in the middle of 2010. That is, of course, a tough recession; but it is not a repeat of the 1930s. Policy decisions do, however, have their effects. For example, in early February 2009, we predicted a "Second Quarter Bounce" long before any green shoots began to be discussed, much less appeared. The reason was the size of the fiscal stimulus plan that had been passed. But because of its inefficient design, we also warned our clients that this might induce a bond market sell-off and that the lack of efficient design would mean that any near-term bounce would likely not lead to a sustained recovery. Thus, the role of history in helping maintain objectivity in any industry is a complicated one.

The way we approach this challenge is to imagine ourselves as future historians writing about the events of the present. This causes us to contemplate an outcome, which we as future historians have the advantage of knowing with 20/20 hindsight, and then work back to establish a chain of events that led to that outcome. When you do that, you have to visualize how something is going to happen and decide whether or not your vision is realistic. If it is not realistic, you reject it. Thus, only a small fraction of the speculative "future histories" one considers actually make it into the range of plausible scenarios. For example, if one imagines a future history of rapid economic expansion in 2010—as the administration and many in the economics profession believe—one has to imagine a sharp decline in the personal saving rate. There is no way to stand in December 2010 with a rapidly growing economy without having had consumers resist raising their savings and choosing to spend instead. Is this plausible? It is certainly possible, but given the widespread wealth destruction and high degree of unemployment-induced economic uncertainty, it is a much less plausible scenario than assuming a further increase in the saving rate. So we tend to differ with most forecasters regarding the speed and timing of the recovery.

This future-history approach doesn't guarantee that you will have picked the right future, but it does facilitate objectivity. Once present-day events occurred that differed from what you imagined, that is, once the world ended up somewhere other than where you thought it was going to end up, you would know that, objectively, you were wrong.

Candor Is Key

It is so important in business to remember that you are not just dealing with economic data and trends; you are also dealing with people. You must be honest with your clients, no matter how unpleasant the news is. Candor requires that you state your objective and independent opinion to someone who may not want to hear it. Your analysis may, in fact, implicitly be telling someone, "You're wrong." What makes candor particularly challenging in the consulting world is that the person to whom you are being candid is paying you.

There are, of course, some obvious pointers on how to deliver the candid but undesirable message. One should always be polite, strive to listen carefully, and remain objective and analytic. Try not to defend your message simply because it is yours, but instead because the facts warrant it. No one should believe that candor is easy. It really depends on the client, and what you may conclude is that your product or service is really not for everyone. One obvious place where candor gets tough is the discussion of politics.

Politics entail risks to our clients; thus, they should receive our best judgment on what the numbers say the outcome of an election is—and what that outcome is likely to mean for policy. Predicting the outcome of an election is very much like economic forecasting; it is data-intensive and requires both independence and objectivity to do it right. We called both the 2004 and 2008 election results almost precisely correctly, erring on the popular vote margin both times by only a few tenths of a percent. In 2008, we missed by a single electoral vote—the first district of Nebraska, which voted for Obama, although the state voted for McCain (we had not broken down the outcome to the congressional district level).

But delivering that result was not easy. Our Democratic clients were none too pleased with our yearlong predictions of the 2004 race, given their distaste for Bush; and our Republican clients were not happy with our view that Obama was going to win easily. There were times during both elections when the polls of the moment were calling the reverse result. But again, future history suggested that looking back from the perspective of after Election Day and trying to chart a path to that outcome made that contrary result implausible.

The Next Phase

The next phase of the economic crisis was the financing phase. Although the economy overall did not deleverage, some leverage was moved from the private sector to the public sector. The lost private sector leverage represented a general recognition of lower asset values—and an offsetting, public sector-financed reduction in liabilities. As a result, the private sector was not made fundamentally better off, in that its net worth did not increase. Instead, the hole that had emerged in its balance sheet was recognized, or partially recognized, and the institutions that faced insolvency issues as a result were rescued by a debt-financed injection of capital from the government. From the point of view of the national balance sheet, the country is therefore poorer.

This reduction in wealth necessitates a slowing of economic activity. It should happen primarily in the consumption spending of the household sector, because this more than any other sector saw a reduction in wealth that was not offset by government. In particular, we anticipate saving rates to continue to increase as households seek to rebuild their balance sheets. By contrast, official forecasts anticipate that the saving rate will fall again and return to the levels seen in the middle of the decade. If those official forecasts turn out to be analytically wrong, then economic growth will face a tremendous headwind going forward—and we should see a subpar economic performance at least through 2010 and possibly longer. So the analytic point for markets should be to determine whether household savings will fall in the face of deteriorating balance sheets and high unemployment, as the administration and most official forecasts presume, or whether it will rise. If officials are wrong and their budgetary and economic projections turn out to be too rosy, the second analytic challenge will be to determine how economic leaders will respond.

Our view is that the household saving rate will ultimately rise to 8 to 10 percent and the unemployment rate will rise to double-digit levels. If this is correct, how then will the administration and other public sector decision makers respond? How will markets react? We anticipate that leaders will use more rhetoric and political management. Of course, as a future historian looking back on the path that produces this outcome, one must remain alert to possible changes that would signal a different outcome.

One such change would be an actual sharp decline in the personal saving rate that many now have built into their forecasts. That would mean more robust economic growth over the near term. Although it would produce real long-term challenges to the country, the temporary relief provided by a lower saving rate would likely take some of the pressure off the political developments described previously. A second such change would be a shift in the balance of decision-making power within the administration away from rhetoriticians and political managers and toward analytic experts.

If history is any guide, there will be a series of major personnel shake-ups over the next couple of years. It will be interesting to see which leadership types gain ground and which lose ground.

Grappling with the Crisis

One of the advantages that our firm offers is that all of the principals at The Lindsey Group have spent time working for different political leaders as well as being involved in financial markets. And with increasing power flowing to Washington, this should prove crucial. Our experience develops a deeply seated sense of realism about leadership. In particular, it emphasizes the point that nobody is perfect. There are two corollaries to this observation about leadership: First, it means that leaders will tend to perform well at some tasks and not so well at others. In general, successful leaders tend to use the skills they have in abundance to compensate for their shortcomings. Second, the universality of imperfection means that when one has a leader who thinks he or she is perfect—or almost perfect—or if there is a media perception that this is the case, mistakes are likely to be made and expectations are almost certain to be disappointed. This is not a disparagement of any particular individual; rather, it is an independent, objective, and candid view of the difficulties leaders are going to have in grappling with the current crisis.

One should start the analysis with leadership style. Of the three types of leadership described here—managerial, rhetorical, and analytic—the current administration appears to have the first two in abundance. The rhetorical powers of President Obama are second to none. He exceeds those of Bill Clinton, and at least rivals those of Ronald Reagan. Many analysts of leadership skills that are required of a President put this rhetorical power as first in importance. After all, President Barak Obama must convince members of Congress and the public at large of the importance of his agenda. There is no doubt that President Obama has done this, given the size of his mandate in November; his ability to produce electoral coattails, which gave his party a very comfortable majority in Congress; and his propensity since the inauguration to turn that majority into legislation.

Indeed, the ability to move legislation through quickly is another reminder of the skills the administration has in political management. Although the president does not appear to manage per se, and instead devotes his time to maximizing the use of his rhetorical skills, he has hired a tremendously successful team of political managers in the likes of Rahm Emanuel, Valerie Jarrett, and David Axelrod. These three were instrumental in his upset victory over Hillary Clinton in the contest for the Democratic presidential nomination, and they ran a virtually flawless general election contest against John McCain. They are people who know how to move the political process to deliver on the rhetorical leadership that is President Obama's strong suit. In addition, they collectively enforce a degree of message discipline over administration personnel that is far greater and more successful than that developed by the Bill Clinton or George W. Bush White Houses (and neither Clinton nor Bush were particularly slackers in this regard).

What is less clear at this point is whether the administration has developed real analytic powers. There is no doubt that they have extremely talented individuals who possess such powers in both the economic and the foreign policy areas. But the balance of power within the administration and the process of decision making is driven far more by the managerial and rhetorical demands of leadership than the analytic. In the economic area, this tendency for rhetoric to get ahead of analysis showed up in the stimulus bill. To their credit, administration officials contacted a good variety of economic forecasters, including me, on the appropriate size of the stimulus package. I concurred on the size that ultimately was proposed: $800 billion. But the administration's analytic work stopped there. It then turned over the crafting of the details of the stimulus bill to the Congress, and more precisely, to the appropriations committees in Congress. These are the reptilian brains of the political process whose single thought is to spend on the projects the members of the committee and their friends want. The result was an absolute disaster: money appropriated to areas that would have little benefit to the economy or job-creation effect. This conclusion was widespread among budget analysts, including the Congressional Budget Office, which noted that the long time lag on spending made this a particularly inefficient piece of "stimulus."

The inefficiency of the stimulus bill and the other spending that has gone through Congress is producing an unintended consequence that is going to drive the economy, markets, and, indirectly, public policy in the months ahead. This inefficiency produces the combination of a weak recovery—particularly on the jobs front—and sharply rising budget deficits. These higher deficits, in turn, put pressure on interest rates. To attract the necessary funds to finance the deficit, rates must rise in order to attract capital from abroad or crowd out private domestic investment or debt-financed consumption.

Leadership in the Financing Phase

Thus, the economics of the financing phase of this crisis is inextricably linked to the political handling of the crisis. In contemplating the likely actions of the administration, it is worth considering how they view themselves—and how their allies view them. The most common phrase used in Washington and in the mainstream media is that they are "pragmatists," a moniker they've earned because they have shown a willingness to compromise. For example, it became obvious on the Cap-and-Trade scheme that the opposition by current emitters of carbon and their customers would block what was basically a "carbon tax" approach. So the administration gave up on collecting revenue from Cap and Trade and used 85 percent of the supposed proceeds as a give back to the polluters who were objecting to the proposal. This is pragmatic, but it has unintended consequences. The $80 billion per year that was expected to be collected—and that was a key part of the president's long-run budget—has just been given away. This only further weakens the analytic position of the fiscal policy position of the country and the administration.

So, pragmatism is not analytical, and it is quite different from realism. A pragmatist is a rhetorical leader or political manager who has been mugged by reality. An analytic realist might have noted the incompatibility of counting on carbon tax revenue that was crafted in a way that would have ensured its political defeat, while a pragmatist plows forward anyway and compromises when forced to.

Apply this pragmatism to the possibility that the economy does not expand as the administration expects because of a household desire to increase savings. The analyst would have a plan B in place.

A pragmatist waits for reality to hit and then deals with it in a way that seems right at the time. The one thing a pragmatist can't do is admit that he or she was wrong and take back what was proposed to try a new approach. Rhetorical and managerial leaders don't do this. Like Chuck Prince, they will keep dancing as long as the music is playing; and if they have enough power, they will do all they can to make sure that the band keeps playing.

This does not mean that they can't adapt or compromise. One obvious possibility would be to go on offense and say that what was done was right, but too small in magnitude, so what is needed is to do more of the same, that is, to use the formidable rhetorical and political management skills of the administration to pass another stimulus bill. A number of analysts, particularly on the left, have already called for doing so. Although this is a possibility, it is unlikely to be the path of least resistance for the political process or for the markets. The markets pose the most obvious impediment. They are already reacting to the massive financing needs that the first stimulus bill and other pieces of legislation created by driving intermediate and long-term interest rates substantially higher. This is crowding out other economic activities and making particular trouble in the bond market. So it would be questionable, to say the least, on economic and financial grounds to simply do more of the same.

But there is a separate political factor that probably blocks exploring this avenue. Politicians respond to the behavioral characteristic of, "if it feels good, do it." Trouble is, this avenue didn't feel so good. In general, the political feedback has been poor, with voters asking tough questions about the inefficacy of what was passed and the "strings" that were attached. Thus, taking the offensive in fiscal matters seems unlikely; a defensive response seems more so.

Economically and in markets, all of this will come together in a reversal of the Great Moderation. That 25-year historical moment increased private risk taking as the perceived riskiness of public decision making declined. The leverage created by that private risk taking and the asset prices supported by it remain in place, but this leverage is inappropriate for the new era. As more power devolves to Washington, the market risks associated with policy formation increase. This means that risk premiums must rise across the board. Equity risk premiums will rise because more of the volatility of economic performance will come from discrete political decisions rather than more gradual market ones. Credit and term structure risk premiums will also rise as uncertainties about future monetary and fiscal policy increase. All things equal, this could also mean a lower equilibrium level for the foreign exchange value of the dollar.

Prospering in this New Economy

As more power is shifted to Washington, the challenge for investors becomes more difficult. Some are advocating a policy of "invest with the government and you can't go broke." This would lead one to put money in the new partly nationalized sectors of the economy, such as the large money center banks, the auto companies, and probably parts of the health care industry. This does not seem like a good way to initiate the financing phase of an economic crisis. Although these firms are surviving because they get money from Uncle Sam, Uncle Sam himself is running out of borrowing capacity. Even if his new wards in the private sector don't go broke, they won't be allowed to be exceptionally profitable either. Those profits will be appropriated to fill other missions that Washington needs accomplished.

The central issue for America will be to pay its bills—particularly its overseas debt. This will mean that America's exporters will have a very important role to fill. The likely decline in global faith in the dollar will help them along. If one thinks about those things in which America already has a comparative advantage—agriculture, aircraft, entertainment, and technology—the new economy will require them to be even more profitable than in the past.

But a broader and more hands-on government will also mean a rollback in the areas of the economy that have benefited from financial intermediation. Home ownership rates are unlikely to regain their recent peaks. Indeed, in terms of metrics like square feet of living space per person, we have probably seen peaks that may never be attained again, or if so, only after decades of recovery. It is worth keeping in mind that the total stock of housing investment did not keep up with depreciation from 1929 through 1945, despite a growing population.

Finance itself is likely to change and become less intermediated. Institutions that were set up to bring borrower and lender together in an increasingly complex financial arrangement have been significantly discredited, because the real value of their involvement generally was less than the fees they charged. In the new economy, we suspect that private arrangements will become more common as entanglement with highly regulated financial intermediaries becomes less attractive. Moreover, given recent institutional failures, traits such as independence, objectivity, and candor will be valued more than marquee names in the intermediation arena.

The new economy will also be one in which new economic leadership will emerge. Although we do not believe that America's best days are behind us, the confluence of rising political control over economic matters in the midst of this financing phase means that near term, the relative economic power of America will wane. Our relationships as a firm reflect this. We are rapidly developing contacts and doing business in South and East Asia and Arabia. It is worth keeping in mind that financial and economic relationships in these areas tend not to be institutionalized, and only lightly intermediated. Trust—and a long experience with the individuals with whom one does business—is vital. It is particularly interesting that what we would have considered an "underdeveloped" financial marketplace in these areas is actually the kind of model to which we will gradually evolve in this financing phase of the crisis.

The greatest question in these areas is whether a dollar-based global economy will continue or whether the whole concept of a pure fiat-money system will also be a casualty of the recent crisis.

Current talk of a "currency basket" replacing the dollar seems misplaced. The problem the dollar has is that it is thought to be subject to political manipulation in order to meet the near-term economic needs of the United States. Substituting a basket of such currencies, each politically manipulated by its own government, hardly seems like a compelling substitute. The more pressing question is whether one of the newly emerging countries decides that it can offer a real competitor to the dollar by moving away from a fiat-based system toward one that represents a more pure store of value. Some form of specie-based currency may turn out to be a real possibility in our new economic era if global faith in the dollar erodes.

2

Steve Forbes

When it comes to the marriage of politics and the economy, Steve Forbes, former presidential candidate; chairman, president, and CEO of Forbes; and editor-in-chief of *Forbes* magazine; is one of the best authorities in the industry. The company's flagship publication, *Forbes,* is the nation's leading business magazine, with a U.S. circulation of 919,742. It has 11 local language editions that reach a worldwide audience of more than 5 million readers. Steve's charisma and economic knowledge are embraced by many around the world.

September 2008 was the culmination of a series of disasters in government policies, starting with the weak-dollar policy of the Bush Administration and the Federal Reserve. The housing bubble would never have reached the size it did had it not been for the Fed's actions. Fannie Mae and Freddie Mac stoked the flames of this crisis with more than $1 trillion in junk mortgage guarantees. This crisis was exacerbated by the government's inconsistency—by first saving the operations of Bear Stearns but then by letting Lehman Brothers, which was infinitely more important and consequential, go under. It was very clear by that infamous September weekend that we were in the midst of a financial panic, the likes of which we had not seen since the 1930s. We had experienced many disasters before, but not on this scale.

The Bush Administration's floundering became clear in the spring of 2008. This continued on into the summer with Fannie Mae, Freddie Mac, and AIG coming under scrutiny. The Administration needed to stop twiddling its thumbs and hoping for the best and needed to take action. But with the failure of Lehman Brothers, it was obvious that President Bush, Treasury Secretary Hank Paulson, and Fed Chairman Ben Bernanke didn't know what they were doing. It was clear that no preparations were made at all, nor did these people understand the utter destructiveness of applying mark-to-market accounting rules to the regulatory capital of banks and life insurance companies. Another policy blunder is the repeal of the uptick rule.* The short selling of securities was banned during the Great Depression for good reason. However, this ban was lifted in 2007. The Securities and Exchange Commission (SEC) is still sitting on this.

* *Author's note:* The uptick rule was adopted by the Securities and Exchange Commission in 1938 and removed in 2007. It prevented the short-selling of securities unless they are on an uptick.

Defining the New Economy

The economy, battered by post-credit crisis 2007 and post–Lehman 2008, is ready to grow again—if the government could just get its act together. Clearly, the Obama Administration does not understand the need for a stable dollar; has no appreciation of the destructiveness of tax increases; is still trying to nationalize health care; is still trying to push cap-and-trade; and still won't ratify new trade agreements such as those with Colombia and South Korea (particularly important because the world is toying with protectionism more and more and the Administration is doing nothing to stop it).

Kick-Starting the New Economy

Short term, the Fed needs to live up to its reputation; that is, it must pump liquidity into mortgage-backed securities and packages of car loans and credit card loans. Although the Fed and the Administration have talked about making these moves, precious little has been done. The Fed's balance sheet is now smaller than it was in December. (See Figure 2.1.)

Figure 2.1 Credit Extended through Federal Reserve Liquidity Facilities

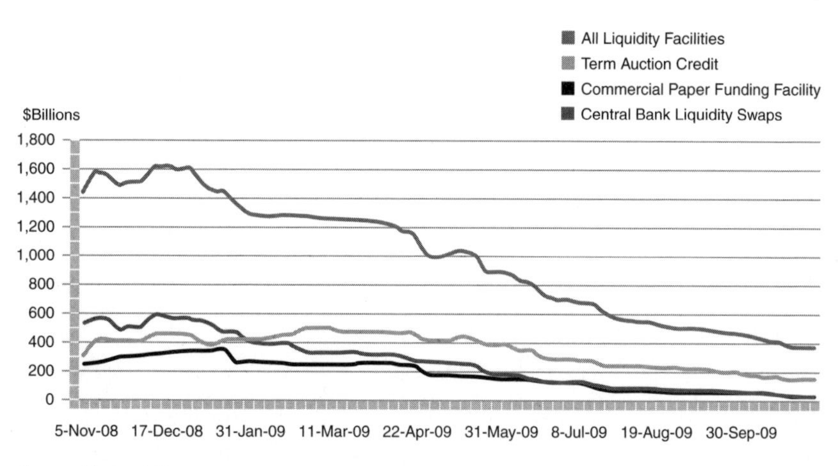

Source: Federal Reserve

Using History as a Guide for the Future

To thrive in this new economy, you have to do two things immediately and simultaneously: tighten your belt in the short term, reducing expenses and reorganizing operations to meet current short-term conditions, and move forward with initiatives and make investments in areas and projects that will build your future.

Forbes magazine had experience with this in 2001. After the events of 9/11 the economy slid into a recession and continued to decline. The advertising business began falling off a cliff. Advertising in *Forbes* decreased by 40 percent. And the company was losing boatloads of money in our new web site venture. We decided nevertheless to continue to pump money into our web site. Other players however, froze and did nothing. When the recovery came in 2003, Forbes.com did magnificently because of the long-term initiatives we already had in place. In fact, in 2003 the web site made more money than the print side of the business. Today, Forbes.com has almost 20 million unique visitors a month. Today, we have to apply the same strategy: coping with the short-term problems while not losing sight of the need to take initiatives for the future.

We are currently launching new tools and resources on the web site while continuing to expand our network, both online and in print. On May 21, 2009, we launched *Forbes* in India, and it is off to a great start. We now have 11 local editions of *Forbes*. In April of 2009, we launched *ForbesWoman* on the Web. This site is devoted to women in business. There is also a publication to go along with the web site. Essentially, we learned that in a down economy you have to both tighten your belt *and* plant seeds for the future, which is tough to do.

Today's economic atmosphere is much more intense. Before this crisis, most people had no doubts about the future of print. People weren't worried about the survival of the banking system. They weren't concerned about what the government was going to do regarding General Motors. But you can't get caught up in just coping with immediate conditions and trying to get by. You also have to plan for the future—only blocking and tackling will not help you grow in times of crisis.

Future of Magazines

Thankfully for our company, magazines are in a different world than newspapers. News is a commodity now, and people want it instantly, searching for it on their handhelds. However, people still do read magazines. Our readership both nationally and overseas has actually never been better, never been higher. When people read magazines, they do so with a different frame of mind; it's a relaxed frame of mind. They like the tactile flexibility of magazines.

Ad spending in the first half of 2009 was terrible and was reminiscent of the tough business climate following 9/11. But earlier, in 2008, Forbes began making positive changes in the way we marketed both the web site and the magazine. We actually integrated the marketing and advertising of both.

Most of the content on our web site does not appear in the magazine. Because the Internet allows for more immediacy, there's a far broader range of content online than is available in a magazine. Video has also become a major component of Forbes.com. In the fall of 2008, we launched a video feature called Intelligent Investing. I sit down with people such as Jack Bogle for a half-hour interview—this has proven to be very popular. You can see the same approach on CNBC.

On the magazine side, we are able to do things graphically and in depth, even though our stories are always short and to the point. Graphics give credibility to a story. The amazing part of this is that even though people go to the Web for quick information, they also go there to get more information on topics they've read about in a magazine.

Looking Ahead to the Future

It is impossible to predict where we will be 10 years from now. No one could have foreseen an event like 9/11, or the massive growth of the Web and the impact it would have on so many industries. We have also seen the rise of such phenomena as social networks, Google, and products like the iPod, as well as the catastrophic economic crisis that began in the summer of 2007.

As long as you maintain the flexibility to adjust and adapt when unforeseen circumstances arise, you can map a long-term strategy to help you reach your business goals. Our strategy is to continue to develop our web site in terms of creating new features and new products, especially proprietary products that increase value. We also own other sites, including Investopedia, and hold a majority in RealClearPolitics, which is a great aggregator of political articles. There is a lot of opportunity to grow. And as I mentioned earlier, we are also expanding overseas—both in print and online.

The relationship between media and culture in other countries is a very sensitive thing. One does not dare develop business in China, for example, without having a local partner there. And until recently India has traditionally been quite restrictive as well. But India changed its rules governing publications in the fall of 2008, a move that enabled *Forbes* to come in as *Forbes India*. We are working with Network18, which is the CNBC affiliate in India.

Whether the medium you use to reach your market is television, radio, print, or online, it is the way you execute your strategy that will ultimately determine your success or failure. There is not one approach that will work for everyone. But in turbulent times, everyone will be up for a while and then down again. In a crisis like this, everyone is going to be hard hit. But when things level out again, there are those who will do well and those who will fall by the wayside.

Edison was right: 1 percent inspiration, 99 percent perspiration.

3

David Malpass

Former chief economist at Bear Stearns and current president of Encima Global, David Malpass, provides a wealth of insight on recently transformed economic policies. In 2005, 2006, and 2007, while at Bear Stearns, Mr. Malpass ranked second in the *Institutional Investor* ranking of Wall Street economists. Prior to his time there, David worked in Washington economic policy positions for nine years. He held several economic positions during the Reagan and Bush Administrations between

(*continued*)

(continued)

February 1984 and January 1993, including serving as deputy assistant treasury secretary for developing nations, deputy assistant secretary of state, Republican staff director of Congress's Joint Economic Committee, and senior analyst for taxes and trade at the Senate Budget Committee.

David worked on a variety of economic, budgetary, and international issues in his government roles: the 1986 tax cut, the Gramm-Rudman budget laws of 1990, several congressional budget resolutions, the savings and loan bailout of the 1990s, the North American Free Trade Agreement (NAFTA), the Brady Plan for developing country debt at the end of the 1980s, and the fast-track trade authority process enacted in 2001. He was a member of the government's Senior Executive Service and testified frequently before Congress. Here, David offers his insight and analysis on global economic and political trends, with investment research spanning equities, fixed income, commodities, and currencies.

In March 2008, the Fed was in rate-cutting mode, which turned out to be a reasonable short-term buying opportunity. Why? Over the decades, situations wherein the monetary policies are loosened have been generally favorable times for investing. Also, investing after crises has, in most cases, made sense for Americans—for example, after 9/11, after Hurricane Katrina, and after the 2007 securitization wipeout, which extended up to the Bear Stearns takeover by J.P. Morgan. Of course, the weak dollar and high oil prices during the summer of 2008 and Lehman Brothers' bankruptcy created a second—and more severe—crisis.

The sector valuations considered most attractive have shifted over the decades. Technology was favored in the 1990s, then financial services through 2006. The August 2007 breakdown of securitization had a very harsh effect on financial services companies. I had a complete change of view to the negative in August 2007 based on the breakdown of how finance was being done. Just as the burst of the NASDAQ bubble in 2001 caused a long-term slow period for technology stocks, the same happened to financial services in August 2007. The crisis was a fundamental negative change for the entire sector. Separately, materials and commodity stocks continued to be very strong through July 2008 based on the weak dollar policy of the United States.

I wrote three articles for the *Wall Street Journal* in late 2007 through March 2008 that criticized the Bush administration's dollar-weakening policy. Although that policy had positive implications for oil, oil stocks, and other commodity stocks, it was detrimental to the rest of the economy due to higher raw materials costs and the inflation impact. Inflation hit 5.6 percent in July 2008, which was very harmful to many sectors.

Markets Post Lehman Brothers

I was surprised and dismayed by the bankruptcy of Lehman Brothers; the market was completely unprepared for that development. It marked a major negative inflection point for the U.S. economy and for the market outlook. The day after Lehman Brothers declared bankruptcy, the commercial paper market stopped functioning. The market between banks for interbank loans stopped functioning. Even nine months later, markets have not fully repaired.

Finding Inflection Points

I try to identify major inflection points in my analysis of the market. During most months of the year, there's not a major change of direction within the market. People are trading week by week within a relatively continuous market, so finding the turning point is a critical issue. After Lehman Brothers' bankruptcy, I took the view that the economy would quickly hit a brick wall. The goal was to make clear in investors' minds the extent of the changes they would see post–Lehman Brothers—and one way to do that was to compare it to the August 2007 inflection point. In August 2007, I had a major conference call where I gave a negative change of view, which was something that was uncharacteristic for me given my usual optimism. I then explained the Lehman Brothers' bankruptcy and the economic downturn would be five to ten times worse than the August 2007 crisis.

New Economy Strategy

From the standpoint of investment strategy, the bankruptcy of Lehman Brothers created the most deeply negative environment that we've had since the Asia crisis in 1998—the deflation crisis that swept the world and lasted through 2002. The normal range for assets allocated to equities is 30 to 60 or 70 percent. After Lehman Brothers declared bankruptcy, people were forced to think in terms of a negative allocation, a "net short" kind of a position to guard against the extent of the economic contraction. Investors are normally optimistic about the long run, which has been an accurate outlook for American investors since 1982. The Volcker-Reagan nexus in 1981 that focused on reducing inflation helped create a basically favorable disinflation environment that lasted until Lehman Brothers declared bankruptcy. After that we found ourselves in an environment where people had to think about being net short—something that's now an available strategy because of the ultrashort exchange-traded funds (ETFs).*

* *Author's note:* ETFs or Exchange Traded Funds are funds that can track a basket of assets like an index fund, a commodity, or an index. It is traded like a stock on a stock exchange. This type of fund gives investors the ability to sell the fund short while having the diversification of owning an index fund. An example of an ETF is the S&P 500 Index, the Spider (SPDR).

We have to identify what exactly caused the downturn in the markets. The cost of capital is higher, the size of government is bigger, and the potential growth of the economy has been reduced. Growth comes from the private sector. The shift toward government dominance of the economy lowers expectations for productivity and Gross Domestic Product (GDP) growth as well as expectations for corporate earnings growth into the future. This will remain so until those factors—the higher cost of capital and the bigger public sector relative to the private sector—can be reversed.

We are in a long-term diminished environment that will take some time to rebuild into another, better earnings environment. The economy hit a brick wall after Lehman Brothers and went into an extended free fall—one that will take a lot of time to recover from. The message to our clients is to not reach too far for the green shoots and to be cautious in their investments given both the Washington policies (which keep getting worse) and the effects in the real economy. For example, the shifting of bank and credit market lending toward the elite and away from small businesses means that the credit allocation function is moving toward larger companies and governments and away from innovation and entrepreneurism. That again signifies that it will take an extended period of time to work this out.

Another observation is that given the distortion of prices that occurred between 2005 and 2007, due to the Federal Reserve's mistakes on interest rates, it will take more time for us to establish a baseline for prices for commodities and other assets within the economy. This means a long period of sorting out price levels, which creates opportunities. The successful stock pickers will find companies that benefit from those price dislocations.

In the first half of 2009, we experienced an almost month-by-month deterioration of the economy as reflected in jobless claims and inability to roll over debt. Neither banks nor credit markets have recovered their full functionality from Lehman Brothers' bankruptcy. Though improving, we are still in an evolving crisis, and it's probably too early to make long-term investment plans. After stock prices fell as severely as they did in February 2009, their valuations were cheap. The problem is that the earnings are going through a fundamental change post–Lehman, so it is still too early to try to buy stocks based on valuation at this point. We are still in that chaotic period after the all-out free fall. People will be more successful in doing value-based investing late in 2009.

4

Jack Bogle

It's my job at CNBC to book the big news makers and to create and produce must-see news events—one of which is the "Squawk Financial Summit." For one hour, we bring some of the biggest Wall Street names on the CNBC program *Squawk Box* to talk about the news of the day and how it is affecting the markets, but more importantly, to look at opportunities. My financial summit comprises mutual fund legend, Vanguard founder, and former CEO Jack Bogle; BlackRock vice chairman and global chief investment officer of equities Bob Doll; bond king PIMCO's managing director Paul McCulley; and strategist and president of Goldman's Global Markets Institute Abby Joseph Cohen.

(*continued*)

(continued)
Jack Bogle is truly one of Wall Street's legends. Bogle founded Vanguard in 1974, and under his leadership the company grew into the second largest mutual fund company in the world. Jack is a no-nonsense kind of guy; he tells it like he sees it.

Today's turbulence reflects in important measure the failure of our commercial and investment banks to consider the extraordinary risks of the securities they were creating and marketing—and earning billions in fees and commissions, even as they were left with tens of billions of dollars, even hundreds of billions, on their own balance sheets. Given Wall Street's ever-pressing need to have something, anything, to sell in the way of "new product," it is hardly surprising that these collateralized debt obligations (CDOs) became ever more complex, with even more deeply concealed risk. In league with rating agencies registered with the Securities and Exchange Commission (SEC)—which were evidently paid some $400,000 for each issue on which they placed their imprimatur—an estimated $1 trillion of new CDOs were created entirely out of subprime mortgages. Although individually these mortgages were of dubious credit quality, the CDOs created various "tranches," with about 75 percent rated top investment grade AAA, on the assumption that any defaults would impair only the lower-rated series. Alchemy? No, lead is still lead, not gold.

Liquidity Puts

How, I wonder (and I'm sure that you wonder too), could these agencies have been so unmindful, so cavalier, so craven about the credit risks that so quickly came home to roost? And how much more is yet to be disclosed about the deteriorating market prices of these complex instruments?

We'll know someday. But we have all heard the sadly informative anecdotes of former chairman of the giant Citigroup Charles Prince on the situation in the summer of 2007, as questions about the propriety of his firm's decision were raised: "As long as the music is playing, you've got to get up and dance. We're still dancing." (Citigroup director Robert Rubin had never heard of the "liquidity put."* As 2007 ended, Citigroup disclosed that they held some $25 billion of these instruments.) For Merrill Lynch, the write-down was $22 billion. Following a long period of cheap credit and rife credit availability—and borrowers with high confidence and low collateral—we are beginning to pay the price, even as our economy itself faces a whole plethora of other risks created by our financial system.

Rise of the Financial System

The rise of the financial sector is one of the seldom-told tales of the recent era. Twenty-five years ago, financials accounted for only about 5 percent of the earnings of the 500 giant corporations that compose the Standard & Poor's (S&P) 500 Stock Index. Fifteen years ago, the financial sector share had risen to 10 percent; then to 20 percent in 1997 and to a near-peak level of 27 percent in 2006. (See Figure 4.1.)

If we add to this total the earnings of the financial affiliates of our giant manufacturers (think General Electric Capital, for example, or the auto financing arms of General Motors and Ford), financial earnings likely exceeded one-third of the annual earnings of the S&P

---

* *Author's note:* A liquidity put is the right of holders in collateralized debt obligation (CDO) to sell back a CDO to its issuer at the original price. In 2007, it was circulated in the news that Citigroup had $25 billion in liquidity puts, which greatly increased their exposure to subprime mortgages.

Figure 4.1 Twentieth Century Stock Returns by the Decade

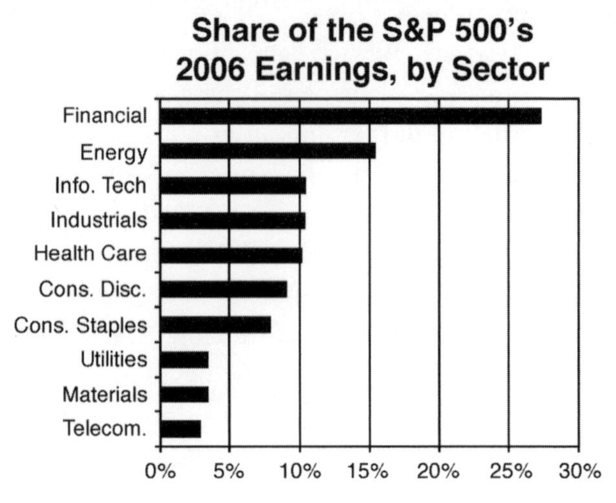

Source: The Vanguard Group

500. In fact, the financial sector is by far our nation's leading generator of corporate profits, larger even than the combined profits of our huge energy and health care sectors, and almost three times as much as either industrials or information technology.

To some degree, of course, the growth of the financial sector reflects not just the rise in demand for financial services (the mutual fund industry is a good example) but also the fact that many privately owned firms have become publicly owned, including investment banking firms, mutual fund managers (once mutual insurance companies), and even our stock exchanges. For example, there were 56 stocks in the S&P financial sector in 1989, including 28 banks; in 2007, there were 92 stocks, but only 26 banks. The combination of public ownership and earnings growth has been dramatic. The earnings of fund manager T. Rowe Price rose from $4 million in 1981 to $582 million in the 12 months ending on June 30, 2007.

In any event, we're moving, or so it seems, toward becoming a country where we're no longer making anything. We're merely trading pieces of paper, swapping stocks and bonds back and forth with one another, and paying our financial croupiers a veritable fortune. We're also adding even more costs by creating ever more complex financial derivatives in which huge and unfathomable risks are being built into our financial system. "When enterprise becomes the bubble on a whirlpool of speculation," as the great British economist John Maynard Keynes warned us more than 70 years ago, the consequences may be dire. "When the capital development of a country becomes a by-product of the activities of a casino, the job (of capitalism) is likely to be ill-done" (1936).

Economic Resiliency

So the risks are high; the uncertainties rife. Yet perhaps we'll make it through. After all, throughout our more than 230-year history, America has always done exactly that. Perhaps, once again, our society and our economy will continue to reflect the resilience that they have demonstrated in the past, often against all odds. And perhaps we'll come to our collective senses and develop the courage to take arms against this sea of troubles I've described and by opposing them, end them. If we do, the stock market will undoubtedly respond and resume the upward course that is based on the intrinsic economic value of business growth.

Successful Investing

Successful investing is not about the stock market, but rather about owning all of America's businesses and reaping the huge rewards provided by the dividends and earnings growth of our nation's—and, for that matter, our world's—corporations. For in the very long run, it is how businesses actually perform that determines the return on our invested capital. Dividend yields, plus earnings growth, account for substantially 100 percent of the return on stocks. Put another way, in the words of Warren Buffett: "The most that owners in the aggregate can earn between now and Judgment Day is what their business in the aggregate earns." Illustrating the point with Berkshire Hathaway—the publicly owned investment company he has run for 40 years—Buffett says, "When the stock temporarily over-performs or under-performs the business, a limited number of shareholders—either sellers or buyers—receive out-sized benefits at the expense of those they trade with. But over time, the aggregate gains made by Berkshire shareholders must of necessity match the business gains of the company."

How often investors lose sight of that eternal principle! Yet the record is clear. History, if only we would take the trouble to look at it, reveals the remarkable, if essential, link between the cumulative long-term returns earned by business—the annual dividend yield plus the annual rate of earnings growth—and the cumulative returns earned by the U.S. stock market. Think about that certainty for a moment. Can you see that it is simple common sense?

Still need proof? Just look at the record since the twentieth century began. The average annual total return on stocks was 9.6 percent, virtually identical to the investment return of 9.5 percent—4.5 percent from dividend yield and 5 percent from earnings growth. That tiny difference of 0.1 percent per year arose from what I call speculative return, depending on how one looks at it. Perhaps it is merely statistical noise, or perhaps it reflects a generally upward long-term trend in stock valuations, a willingness of investors to pay higher prices for each dollar of earnings at the end of the period than at the beginning.

Emotional Investing

Stock market returns sometimes get well ahead of business fundamentals (as in the late 1920s, the early 1970s, and the late 1990s). But it has been only a matter of time until, as if drawn by gravity, they soon return back to earth (as in the mid-1940s, the late 1970s, and the 2003 market lows). (See Figure 4.2.)

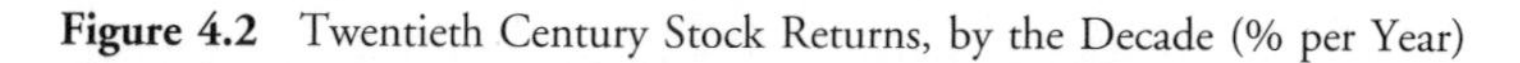

Figure 4.2 Twentieth Century Stock Returns, by the Decade (% per Year)

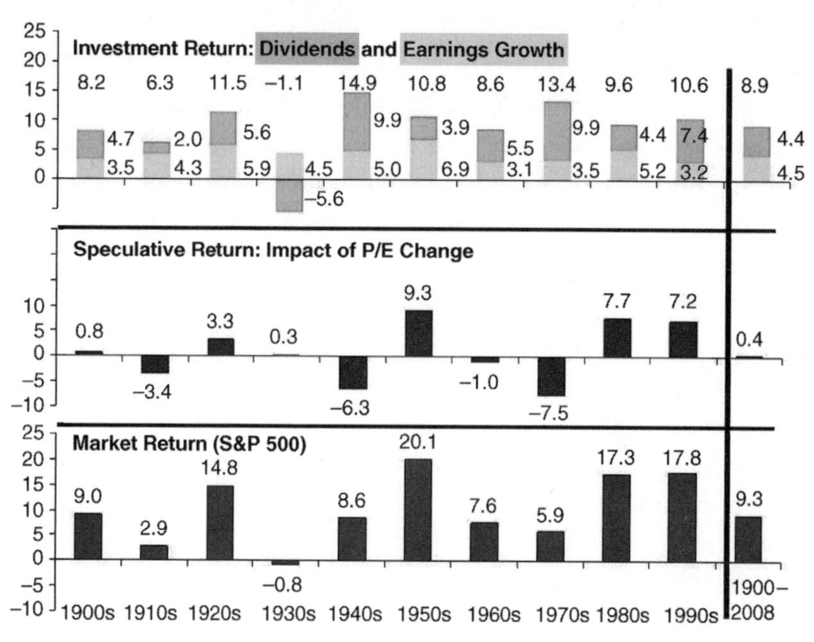

Source: The Vanguard Group

In our foolish focus on the short-term stock market distractions of the moment, we, too, often overlook this long history. We ignore the fact that when the returns on stocks depart materially from the long-term norm, it is rarely because of the economics of investing—the earnings growth and dividend yields of our corporations. Rather, the reason that annual stock returns are so volatile is largely because of the emotions of investing.

We can measure these emotions by the price-to-earnings (P/E) ratio, which represents the number of dollars investors are willing to pay for each dollar of earnings. As investor confidence waxes and wanes, P/E multiples rise and fall. When greed holds sway, we see very high P/E ratios. When hope prevails, P/E ratios are moderate. When fear is in the saddle, P/E ratios are very low. Back and forth, over and over again, swings in the emotions of investors momentarily derail the long-range upward trend in the economics of investing.

Although the prices we pay for stocks often lose touch with the reality of corporate values, in the long run, reality rules. So, although investors seem to intuitively accept that the past is inevitably a prologue to the future, any past stock market returns that have included a high speculative stock return component are a deeply flawed guide to what lies ahead. To understand why past returns do not foretell the future, we need only the words of John Maynard Keynes written 70 years ago: "It is dangerous . . . to apply to the future inductive arguments based on past experience, unless one can distinguish the broad reasons why past experience was what it was."

But if we can distinguish the reasons the past was what it was, then, we can establish reasonable expectations about the future. Keynes helped us make this distinction by pointing out that the state of long-term expectation for stocks is a combination of enterprise ("forecasting the prospective yield of assets over their whole life") and speculation ("forecasting the psychology of the market") (*The General Theory*, Chapter 12). I'm well familiar with those words; 55 years ago, I incorporated them in my senior thesis at Princeton University, written (providentially for my lifetime career that followed) on the mutual fund industry. It was titled *The Economic Role of the Investment Company.*

After almost 55 years in this business, I have little conviction about how to forecast these swings in investor emotions, nor can I predict when they will occur. However, it is clear that when P/E ratios are high (say, above 25), they are apt ultimately to decline; and when they are low (say, below 12), they are apt ultimately to rise. But largely because the arithmetic of investing is so basic, I can forecast the long-term economics of investing with remarkably high odds of success. Why? Simply, it is investment returns—the earnings and dividends generated by American business—that are almost entirely responsible for the returns delivered in our stock market. Put another way, while the momentary prices we pay for stocks are often out of touch with reality—the intrinsic values of our corporations—in the long run, is based on reality.

My advice to you is to ignore the short-term noise of our emotions reflected in our financial markets and instead focus on the productive long-term economics of our corporate businesses. Shakespeare could have been describing the inexplicable hourly and daily—sometimes even yearly or longer—fluctuations in the stock market when he wrote, "[It is] like a tale told by an idiot, full of sound and fury, signifying nothing." The path to investment success is to get out of the expectations market of stock prices and cast your lot with the real market of business. Simply heed the timeless distinction made by Benjamin Graham, legendary investor, author of *The Intelligent Investor,* and mentor to Warren Buffett. He was right on the money when describing the essential reality of investing: "In the short run the stock market is a voting machine . . . (but) in the long run it is a weighing machine."

Riding Out the Risk

Let me conclude by acknowledging that I'm conservative, and well . . . getting on in years. I've followed my own advice and am about 80 percent in bonds and 20 percent in stocks—all Vanguard and overwhelmingly in index funds. But each of us is different. So even if risks are high and uncertainties abound, we must consider not only the probabilities of our investment decisions but the consequences that we face if we are wrong. This, of course, is the famous Pascal Wager, conceived as a bet on whether or not God exists. (Pascal concluded that, considering the consequences, the safer bet was that He existed.) As Peter Bernstein explained the wager, "considering the consequences of being wrong is essential in decision-making under uncertainty." So I urge you all not only to weigh the probabilities of where our markets and our economy are headed in this age of turbulence and uncertainty, but also to weigh the consequences to your own portfolios if you are wrong. If you follow these rules, you'll be able to ride out today's risks and uncertainties with favorable results.

5

Bob Doll

Bob Doll, vice chairman and global chief investment officer of equities of BlackRock, is a *Squawk Box* regular at CNBC and key member of the "Squawk Box Financial Summit," as well as many of our market segments. At BlackRock, Bob manages the flagship Large Cap Series Funds, is a member of the firm's executive committee, and served a term on the board of directors from 2006 through February 2009. Before the merger of BlackRock with Merrill Lynch Investment Managers (MLIM) in 2006, Bob served as president and chief investment officer of MLIM. He was also previously the chief investment officer of Oppenheimer Funds.

On *Squawk Box,* we have referred to Bob as "the trillion dollar man," because he and the other portfolio managers at BlackRock collectively manage over $1.3 trillion in client assets. The financial crises of 2008 and 2009 have challenged Bob and his colleagues, as never-before-seen

(*continued*)

(continued)
market conditions threw the world into unprecedented turmoil. The strategies that Bob discusses in his story are what he credits for his company's continued success.

In retrospect, I think we first realized that we were at the beginning of something serious in early 2008. I was taking part in one of BlackRock's daily research calls, where all portfolio teams across all disciplines and all geographic regions discuss common factors affecting our markets. For some time, we had been hearing our fixed-income teams talk about problems in credit markets, and we had begun to see some subprime mortgage problems emerge. I remember saying that equity markets had not been reflecting these problems. Prices weren't going up any-more, but they weren't yet dropping significantly either. We had no inkling in any way, shape, or form that it would get as bad as it did—or that a massive recession had already begun. We did, however, start to recognize that credit was a problem, acknowl-edged that it was probably going to get worse before it got better, and surmised that credit issues were likely to keep the economy from growing. Following those realizations, we began to reduce our positions in financials. We started rotating out of cyclicality, and we lowered the beta in our portfolios. Of course, we would have done much more of this if we had had a clue as to how bad it was going to get. But, at least at the margin, those were the strategies we began using in our portfolios as we began to convey a more cautious message to our clients.

It wasn't until the summer of 2008 that we started having some real issues. At that point, it had become clear that the credit issues that our fixed-income teams had been talking about for some time were threatening global market stability. In July and August 2008, we saw some of the credit problems emerge. The markets were not operating normally, the Fed was forced to take action, and the equity markets began having more significant setbacks. That was the point at which our clients began wondering, "Hey, what's really going on here?" I don't recall many of them asking us a lot of questions in the first half of 2008; that occurred more frequently during the summer, when markets were significantly affected. I remember that even as recently as Labor Day in 2008 there was a widespread debate—both within BlackRock and among investors in general—as to whether the United States (and the rest of the world) would experience a recession.

By that point, of course, we had seen the collapse of Bear Stearns, but this was still well before Lehman Brothers declared bankruptcy. In retrospect, it's clear that the collapse of Lehman Brothers marked a critical inflection point; and following the collapse, the economy seemed to go from not so healthy to downright sick.

From Waterfall Decline to Base Building

We came to realize very quickly that the mood had shifted. Words such as *depression, defaults,* and *bankruptcies* became a part of our daily conversations as we discussed our portfolios. As the equity markets began their September/October 2008 meltdown, we were wondering how far and how fast the markets would drop. We have all lived through bear markets; typically, bear market declines of 50 percent take a couple of years to develop, but this decline happened in a single year. This bear market was fast, and it was brutal. Along the way, a number of important lows were hit, first on October 10 and then on November 21. At each point, as portfolio managers, we were asking, "Is this the end? Are stocks now cheap enough to warrant buying, or will markets go even lower?"

Since stocks peaked in the fall of 2007, each new low was accompanied by an increase in the new low list on the New York Stock Exchange (NYSE). On the afternoon of Thursday, October 9,

Figure 5.1 Standard & Poor's 500 Index

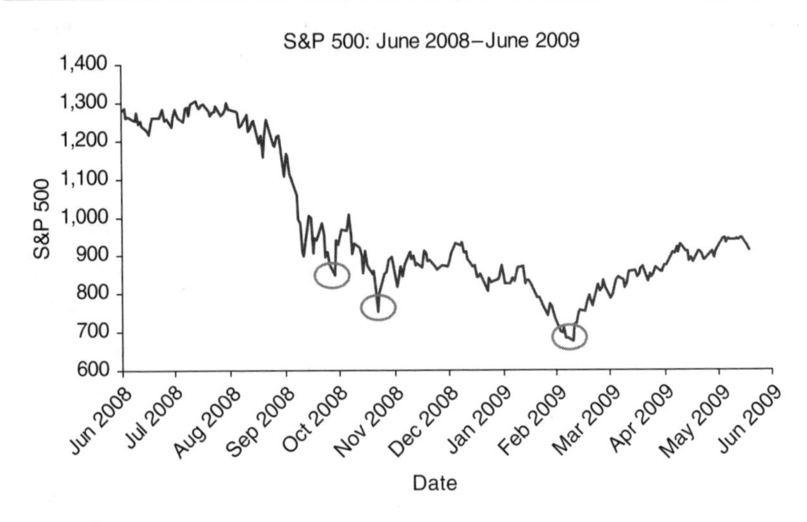

Source: BlackRock

2008, we started seeing some extremely heavy selling and the market was in capitulation mode as people were beginning to give up. The next day, the new low list on the NYSE reached 1,860 stocks—the biggest new low list we had ever seen. Following that low, the market did what it always seems to do during bear markets—it bounced, tried to stabilize, failed, and moved lower.

By November 21, the Standard & Poor's (S&P) 500 Stock Index was down almost another 100 points from its October 10 low, meaning that stocks had dropped approximately 15 percent in five weeks. Significantly, however, the new low list shrunk in half. There's an old saying that you never hear the bell ringing at the bottom; but I remember thinking that on November 21, we may have heard something. The new low pattern had changed, and I think it was a signal.

At the time, we postulated that the "waterfall decline" pattern that had been in place for several months was about to change into a months' long, sideways "base-building" pattern, marked by high levels of volatility. And that's exactly what happened. From

November 21 to early January, the stock market had quite a run to the upside and appreciated by more than 20 percent. At the time, some people thought that the worst was behind them, but stocks then sank further and the S&P reached a new bottom of 666 on March 6, 2009. From that point, stocks began a rebuilding process, and by the end of March, we had begun to believe that the March 6 low would, in fact, mark the ultimate low for the bear market.

Looking Ahead: Deflation versus Reflation

Determining the future course of action of the stock market is obviously a difficult proposition, but it is something that we believe is important to do to help guide our investment decisions. In addition, our clients always want to hear our thoughts on where markets are going. So at the start of every year, we develop a series of 10 predictions covering our forecasted views of the economy, the markets, and factors that may affect our investment portfolios. For 2009, we expanded that list to 12 predictions given the number of issues facing investors. (See Figure 5.2.)

When we develop these predictions, we typically try to find a unifying theme that helps tie them all together. For 2009, the main theme was the tug-of-war between deflation and reflation. Deflationary forces first emerged with the implosion of low-quality mortgages—a contagion that eventually spread to all mortgages and then to debt markets in general. Likewise, the deflation contagion spread to all markets around the world as we saw massive declines in residential real estate, commodity prices, equity prices, and, finally, economic growth.

Reflationary policies were a direct response to these deflationary factors. Policy makers around the world began to enact widespread monetary and fiscal stimulus measures to try to rescue us all from the mess that we had gotten ourselves into. The debate became:

Figure 5.2 2009 Predictions

1. The U.S. economy faces its first nominal GDP decline in 50 years.
2. Global growth falls below 2% for the first time since 1991.
3. Inflation falls close to zero in many developed countries, but widespread deflation is avoided.
4. The U.S. Treasury curve ends 2009 higher and steeper than where it began.
5. Earnings fall by a double-digit percentage again in 2009, the first back-to-back years since the 1930s.
6. High-yield, municipal, and investment-grade corporate bond spreads narrow in 2009.
7. U.S. stocks record a double-digit percentage gain in 2009.
8. U.S. stocks outperform European stocks while emerging markets outperform developed ones.
9. Energy, Health Care, and Information Technology to outperform Utilities, Financials, and Materials.
10. Stock market volatility remains elevated as periodic double-digit percentage rallies and declines occur.
11. Oil and other commodities bottom and move higher by year-end as emerging market economies begin to recover.
12. The U.S. Federal budget deficit soars past $1 trillion as the government continues to grow.

The opinions presented are those of Bob Doll, as of June 2009, and may change as subsequent conditions vary.
Source: BlackRock

"Which will win? Reflation or deflation?" Our answer to the question was—and is—that although reflation and deflation will each win some battles, in the end, reflation should eventually win the war.

Reaching a Bottom

In our minds, this deflation versus reflation discussion was directly related to the question of whether or not we had seen the true bottom in stocks for this cycle. The worst period for the markets occurred in early 2009 amid the widespread debates over the proper role of government in solving the banking crisis. There was an intense fear that the federal government would nationalize significant segments of the nation's banking system. There was also a great deal of confusion regarding what the Federal Reserve, the Treasury, Congress, and the Obama administration were going to do to tackle all of the problems affecting the markets.

It was at the height of this uncertainty that the S&P dropped to that 666 level. That was when we began to see some additional clarity emerge about the Fed's mortgage purchase program, the Treasury's Public-Private Investment Program, as well as signs that the worst of the recession may have passed. Given this backdrop, stocks surged approximately 50 percent in the subsequent months. Clearly, stocks had entered into oversold territory and were pricing in a more negative environment than probably existed. In retrospect, it seems that an S&P of 666 was discounting a depression scenario, which became clear, would not be the case. What we were facing was more of a nasty recession, and one that we now believe has ended.

The question still remains whether the post-March 2009 environment is more of a bear market rally or a new bull market. The answer depends to a large degree on your definition. If by "bull market" you mean that stocks have to reach a new all-time high, then no, we don't expect the current rally to drive the S&P above the 1,500 mark any time soon. In the short term, the 50 percent rise may have overshot the mark a bit and markets may have gotten ahead of themselves; but over the long term, we don't believe we have seen the end of what we are viewing as a cyclical bull market. There is still a lot of cash on the sidelines, and many investors are still looking for entry points to the market, which we believe provides a favorable backdrop for the market's long-term prospects. Looking back to the predictions we discussed earlier, you will see that one of them calls for a double-digit percentage increase for the S&P 500 Index this year. In March, it appeared there was little chance of getting this one right, but as the year gets closer to a close, we are quite confident that we will score this one in the "correct" column. While we would not be surprised to see some sort of market correction occur at any point, we remain optimistic that stocks will end 2009 with double-digit percentage gains.

The Road to Recovery

Given that we now believe the recession has ended and are expecting a double-digit rise in the S&P 500 Index in 2009, the natural question to ask is, "What will this recovery look like?" First, we expect the economic recovery to be slow and below trend. There is still a massive amount of deleveraging that has to happen on the parts of both the consumer and the financial system, which we believe will prevent a quick return to robust growth levels.

From an equity market perspective, it is also important to recognize that the recent rally has been uneven. Lower-quality, more cyclical investments have drastically outperformed, and higher-quality companies have lagged. This trend is not sustainable. A continuation of the rally will require a broadening in terms of sectors and individual names. These are a few of the main reasons we expect to see some pending consolidation, which would hopefully give the markets a chance to regroup before resuming a more broad-based upturn.

Taking a look at some similar historical time periods can also help provide some perspective on what we're looking for in the

Figure 5.3 S&P 500 History Table

Five-Year Periods of Negative Returns		
	Return	**Next Five Years**
1927–1931	**−5.1%**	**22.5%**
1928–1932	**−12.5%**	**14.3%**
1929–1933	**−11.2%**	**10.7%**
1930–1934	**−9.9%**	**10.9%**
1937–1941	**−7.5%**	**17.9%**
1970–1974	**−2.4%**	**14.8%**
1973–1977	**−0.2%**	**14.1%**
1998–2002	**−0.6%**	**12.8%**
	Average	**14.8%**
	Worst	**10.7%**

Source: SBBI 2006 Yearbook

Past performance is no guarantee of future results. It is not possible to invest directly in an index. Performance is represented by SBBI's Large Company Stocks (1926–1955) and the S&P 500 Index (1956–2008), a market capitalization-weighted index which measures price movements of the common stock of 500 large US companies with leading industries.

markets over the longer term. (See Figure 5.3.) Since the Great Depression, there have been nine 5-year time periods—many of which overlap—in which U.S. stocks experienced negative returns. It seems quite likely that when we update this chart in 2010, we'll add a tenth, since the S&P 500 Index will almost certainly be negative from 2004 to 2009.

The important point about this data is what happens in the five-year periods following these downturns. In each case, stocks were up by double-digit percentages. Although we have no way of knowing for certain what the next five years will hold, it is likely that the environment will look a lot more like the right side of this chart than the left.

When Flat Isn't Flat

There is another way to look at the markets through a historical lens that can also provide some perspective for today's investors. Many investors remember the 1970s as a "lost decade" for stocks; and indeed, between 1966 and 1982, the U.S. stock market was essentially flat. (See Figure 5.4.) Is it possible that we could experience another flat 16-year period? We believe it is and argue that it is certainly a possibility that we're in the midst of one right now.

For the sake of argument, let's assume that the tech bubble peak in 2000 was the beginning of another flat 16-year period. (See Figure 5.5.) From that point, we had a three-year bear market that lasted until 2003; a four-year bull market that ended in October 2007 and that brought stocks to a slightly higher level than where they were in 2000; and then the intense and rapid collapse of our current situation. In this scenario, then, we would be just past the mid-point of our 16-year period. From a return perspective, however, we would need to experience an average annual return of 12.8 percent for stocks to return to 2000 levels by 2016. The

Figure 5.4 Dow Jones Industrial Average 1966–1982

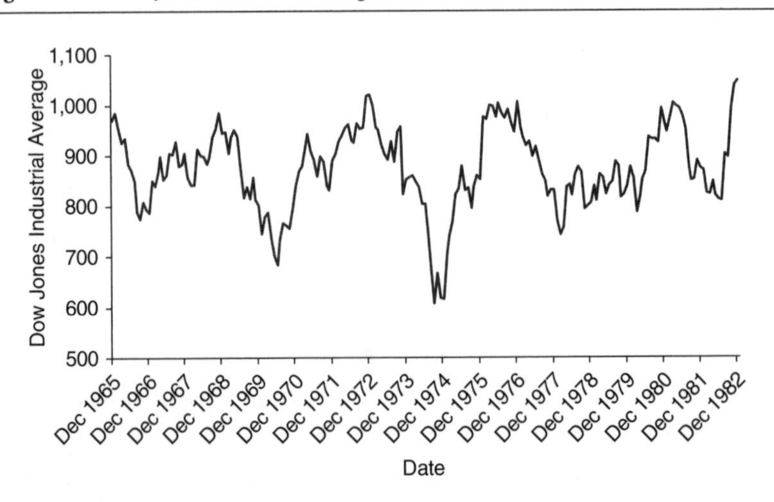

Source: BlackRock

Figure 5.5 16 Flat Years: Can It Happen Again?

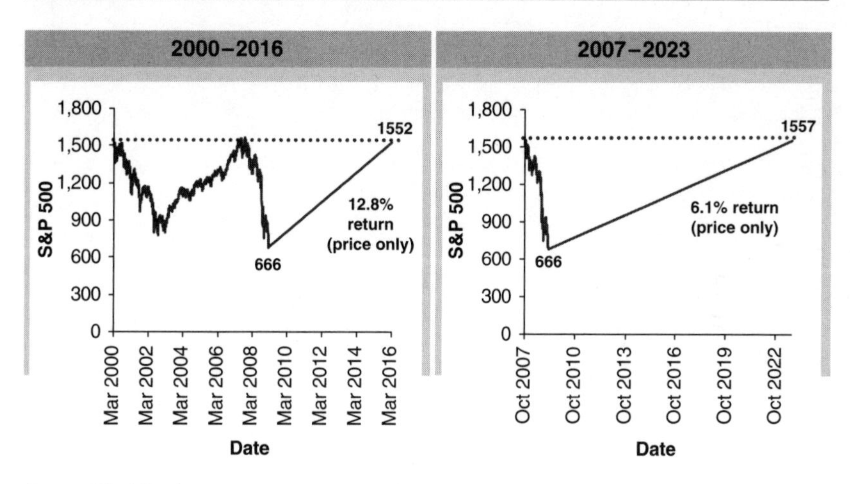

Source: BlackRock

point here is that although history would record the period from 2000 to 2016 as a flat environment in which stocks went nowhere, investors who were able to enter or reenter the markets in 2009 would have enjoyed some excellent returns.

6

Abby Joseph Cohen

Rounding out the "Squawk Box Financial Summit" is senior Investment strategist and president of the Global Markets Institute at Goldman Sachs, Abby Joseph Cohen. Abby started her career as an economist for the Federal Reserve Board in Washington, DC, and then worked for major financial firms as an economist and quantitative strategist. She joined Goldman Sachs in 1990 and was the firm's chief U.S. investment strategist for many years; she was regularly ranked as the top strategist on Wall Street. Her role gradually shifted in the mid-2000s as

(*continued*)

(*continued*)
she assumed increasing responsibilities for the firm's research on long-term issues affecting the economy and markets, including public policy. These have included demographics, pensions, long-term saving, accounting, health care, and climate change. In late 2007, she became president of the Global Markets Institute, the firm's internal think tank. In 2008, her protégé, David Kostin, became Goldman's U.S. stock market strategist. Abby continues to be one of the most quoted financial experts in the field and provides us with her opinion on the economy of late.

The story—at least for me and others at Goldman Sachs—began well before September 2008. Our research began to identify potential anomalies, especially in some credit markets, in late 2005. In fact, the year-ahead reports that we prepared for clients in 2005 and 2006 indicated areas where we thought there were imbalances, especially in the mispricing of risk and in unsustainable growth in some sectors of the economy. For example, we noted some concerns about segments of the household sector, which included the deterioration of the average balance sheet for families; recognizing that overspending and excessive borrowing were occurring in some income categories. This was particularly the case for middle-income and lower-middle-income households for whom inflation-adjusted income growth had been stagnant for several years but whose spending rose, fueled by rising debt levels. Our economics team was also concerned about some housing markets, such as those in areas of notable inward migration, like the Sunbelt region of the Southwestern United States.

Much of my work tries to integrate the economic environment with the performance of financial markets. In combination with my early training on the quantitative side, this means that we try to approach market analysis in a disciplined way. We apply our mathematically based valuation tools to equity markets, fixed-income markets, and other investment categories. At year-end 2005, we expressed concern that lower-quality bonds were offering yields that were too low relative to higher-quality issues. Investors were not getting the usual extra yield, or risk premium, for holding securities of lower-quality issuers. For example, lower-rated corporate bonds often sold at yields not much above those of highly rated bonds. This raised some yellow flags because you would normally expect a riskier issuer to pay more to borrow those funds. Stated differently, the prices of the lower-rated bonds were too high. In addition, others at the firm who looked at mortgage securities were concluding that a similar situation had developed in those markets. Many borrowers with poor credit ratings had access to debt at low rates that seemed out of kilter with the risk being taken on by the lenders. We tracked these apparent discrepancies in 2006 and 2007 and concluded that the mispricing was becoming more intense. Among the concerns was the potential impact of the economic slowdown that we expected to occur. The view of our economics team was that the gross domestic product (GDP) would be much weaker in 2008 than consensus projections indicated.

Staying Ahead of the Curve

We routinely try to find holes in our forecasts. By the end of 2007, we were actively discussing many alternative scenarios, some of them quite ugly. Our research teams were assigning increasingly higher probabilities to the likelihood of a recession. In early 2008, the official Goldman Sachs forecast changed to an outright recession. We thought that a sharp downturn with the ferocity that ultimately developed was a possibility, but not the most likely outcome.

Here's an important point: Our economists were concerned very early about many issues that ultimately unfolded in unpleasant ways. Even so, the magnitude of the recession and the severity of the financial market dislocations were surprising. For example, we had expected problems in the mortgage finance markets. We had expected problems in the housing market. We had expected a moderate recession. But we did not foresee the freezing of financial markets or the sharp drop in economic activity. We became more concerned in March 2008, at the time of the failure of Bear Stearns. The dearth of liquidity during that period was an indication of how quickly some markets could stop functioning in a normal way. We became more alarmed in the summer of 2008.

September Meltdown

Although our analytical teams were prepared for a moderate recession, the market developments in September 2008 were more extreme than most had expected. Simply stated, both equity and fixed-income markets were no longer functioning properly. There was little if no liquidity, and buyers and sellers had difficulty finding suitable transaction prices.

We do a lot of scenario analysis in which we try to stress our conclusions by exploring the outcomes of tough and out-of-consensus assumptions. This testing technique has become increasingly common. Indeed, the recently concluded stress tests for the nation's largest banks used this approach of assuming an unfriendly operating environment to gauge the impact on the banks' soundness. As analysts using this "kick the tires" process, we consciously try to identify assumptions and scenarios that are different from the base case that we believe to be most likely. In September 2008, economic and market developments were moving along the lines of the ugliest alternative scenarios that we had considered. The gloomy scenarios that we had thought were possible, but unlikely, had become probable. Many people around the firm deserve praise for responding to the shifting situation as quickly as they did. The difficult circumstances in September and October included the seizing up of money markets and other fixed-income markets. Volatility rose to exceptionally high levels for both bonds and stocks, roughly five times normal.

Handling Intense Situations

Goldman Sachs is a large firm, with several different divisions. I work in the Global Investment Research division, and we are kept apart from many other commercial activities that are occurring within the firm. We focus on providing analysis and projections to our clients. During the crisis in 2008 to 2009, our research teams around the world moved quickly to adjust forecasts and recommendations to clients. We vigorously tracked and reported on market developments during the intense volatility and confusion of the period. Some of our internal heroes were in our treasury and controllers' functions, people who had responded quickly to the market dislocations.

Nimble

During the market tumult, it became clear that certain assets were not worth as much as investors, lenders, or market makers had previously thought. Goldman Sachs did not wait to write down the value of these assets; we adhered closely to mark-to-market accounting. Although this sounds like a technicality or boring detail, it is an essential component of being nimble. I would equate mark-to-market accounting to sending the canary into the coal mine. We mark to market on a continuous basis. We don't wait till the end of the month; we don't wait until the end of the week; and in some cases, we don't even wait until the end of the day. If we see that an asset has lost value, we mark it down.

Being nimble on accounting also allowed us to be nimble in responding to the market distress in September. In hindsight, everything is simple and easy to see. A critical factor that distinguished some firms during the worst of the financial crisis was not whether they anticipated all the problems, but how quickly they reacted once these problems surfaced.

In Global Investment Research, our focus was on working with our clients and developing a steady stream of analysis during the rapidly changing period. Our industry analysts, that is, those responsible for analyzing specific industries and companies, were often substantially ahead of others in adjusting their earnings estimates and recommendations on buying and selling specific securities. This was also the case for our colleagues who prepare credit research, that is, research on corporate fixed income based on the fundamentals of the underlying companies issuing the bonds.

In general, we took a very conservative approach toward ownership of equities and other corporate securities during this period. This was not based on the downward price momentum but on the deteriorating fundamental performance of the underlying companies. In a deep recession, what were their revenues likely to be? What about their earnings? Cash flow?

My colleague Michael Moran has done an enormous amount of detailed work on the impact of the financial crisis on corporate accounting, including the pension status at major U.S. companies as a consequence of economic and financial market weakness. And there are other issues; for example, what happens to balance sheets? Or to the impairment of goodwill? One positive outcome of the disruption of the past couple of years has been the recognition that the quality and timeliness of data reported on balance sheets and income statements is critical and that effective investment decision making is linked to good understanding of accounting. Not surprisingly, accounting has long been an area of emphasis for us in Global Investment Research.

Be Out of Consensus, If Appropriate

We were also helped by our readiness to take views that were out of consensus, if that's where our research led us—something that our senior managers encouraged. Often, analysts will not wander too far from the conceived wisdom of the crowd, but such consensus views are already largely baked into the stock market and other financial asset prices. Research analysts can provide real value when they start from scratch, using primary data sources, to develop differentiated conclusions in which they have confidence. This applies not just to equity-oriented research but also to credit research. Much of the market disruption in 2007 to 2008 was linked to credit, and it was extraordinarily useful to have internal expertise. The credit team helped us to better and more quickly understand the dimensions of the systemic problems that had developed.

This has been an extraordinary period, with the most severe part starting in September 2008. There have been extreme market moves, extreme shifts in the U.S. and global economies, and major political changes. The 2008 U.S. presidential election has been followed by a series of policy initiatives that could mark significant changes in several areas, including energy, climate, health care, and financial regulation.

We're trying to anticipate the longer-term implications of the economic and credit crisis. Although we recognize that there is still much to be done before there is a return to "normal," we must also recognize that there will likely be a new normal. Among the factors to monitor will be: (1) the role of the United States in the global economy and financial markets; (2) sources of domestic economic growth, especially as the household savings rate has risen; and (3) investor confidence in the proper functioning of markets. Our research focus will be on the longer view, trying to ignore the noise of short-term market developments.

Managing Clients' Expectations

My professional goal is to be helpful to clients by conveying an understanding of economic and market prospects based on the best available analysis. Although it may be entertaining to provide provocative or amusing statements, it is more meaningful to share insights, concerns, and conclusions. Perhaps the most important key to success is to correctly identify the critical variables, those factors that will ultimately drive the economy and markets. Some investors get caught up in trying to forecast many data points with false precision. It is better to identify and emphasize the few factors that will really matter and concentrate on why they are important and the ways in which they are linked.

Many of our clients aim to take a long-term view, perhaps because their needs are also long term. These clients include corporations, pension funds, and charitable institutions and their endowments. We guide them, not in terms of trading tactics between now and next Tuesday, but on how they might think about broad changes in the structure of the global economy (for example, the increased importance of the BRIC nations [Brazil, Russia, India, and China]) and the structure of global capital markets (for example, the impact of multilateral financial regulation on cross-border flows).

We think that the recession ended in the summer of 2009; and our research analysts at Goldman Sachs are actively contemplating some of the changes that may follow during the recovery. For example, our economics teams are analyzing issues such as the relative growth rates of different nations and the likely consequences for foreign trade, protectionism, and currencies. Prior to the crisis, we had already begun work on the longer-term trends likely to evolve in the U.S. economy in the coming decade. It is possible that responses to the crisis may result in faster progress on several fronts than would have occurred without the catalyst of difficult economic times. Important examples include moves toward greater energy efficiency and faster development of alternative energy sources.

We've done much work for the past decade on energy, climate change, and environmental factors, throughout Goldman Sachs. Many clients greeted our initial work with yawns of disinterest. It's been fascinating to watch the explosion in interest now expressed by investors and corporations alike. Over the past couple of years, the debate over climate change has come to life, and has switched from "Is it real?" to "What should we do?" Congress is considering serious new legislation in 2009. Venture capitalists have shifted their attention to energy efficiency and climate remediation. Many pension sponsors and not-for-profit endowments are anxious to allocate funds to assets that demonstrate good environmental, social, and governance citizenship (ESG citizenship).* Another long-term topic of our research has been health care expenditures, including the post-retiree obligations paid for by corporations and the government. The impact at the federal government level is notable because of Medicare; these liabilities may prove to be four to seven times larger than those of Social Security. Also of concern is the underfunding of the post-retirement plans for state and local government employees. Corporate plans seem to be better funded, with notable exceptions in industries that are in duress, such as the auto industry. This issue has now come to the forefront due to the Obama administration's proposed overhaul of health care, and it has been exacerbated by the problems faced by autoworkers and others who are concerned about their health care coverage now as well as at retirement.

---

* Environmental, social, and governance citizenship or ESG Citizenship is investing in funds that are socially responsible such as investing in green technologies or lowering your company's carbon footprint. In addition to environmental issues, corporate governance and social issues are also part of an ESG business model.

Many state and local governments today are facing significant financial problems because of the cyclical downturn. A major recession means lessened tax revenues and increased costs as countercyclical spending programs, such as unemployment insurance, kick in. But even past the recession, these long-term retirement obligations may represent a significant burden.

Even if GDP turns positive in the near future, the labor markets may remain weak for an extended period. The unemployment situation may continue to create dramatic difficulties for many families and the communities in which they live. Is there a possible silver lining to this crisis? Before we explore that, let's understand that, due to unemployment and stagnant wages, the discomfort will continue for many families for some time to come.

Using a Crisis to Your Advantage

Many people are now paraphrasing White House Chief of Staff Rahm Emmanuel's comment about not "wasting a crisis." Several companies, not-for-profit institutions, and other organizations are using this difficult time to identify their core missions. Many are seeking to focus on narrower but more achievable goals. Even those organizations not facing existential risk view the current environment as an opportunity to identify and emphasize comparative advantages and strengths. This is ultimately for the good.

Classical economists like Joseph Schumpeter viewed periods of economic duress as opportunities. His term was *creative destruction,* a time in which activities that were of only marginal benefit do not survive. It is possible for institutions to redirect resources, capital, and, very importantly, people into other activities that could create better growth. To accomplish this as a nation, additional attention should be paid to education and retraining of workers, especially those who are currently unemployed or underemployed. We recently published a research report showing that middle-income wages in the United States stopped growing several years ago, at about the time the average level of education attainment stopped rising.

Investing in Green

The economic and market crises have set the stage for more thoughtful discussions about sustainable growth policies. We see notable opportunities for economic growth and investment returns in the related categories of energy efficiency and broadened use of renewable energy sources. The United States is the world's largest user and importer of energy. This has implications for our foreign policy, and our potential vulnerability is decreased by increased energy independence. These issues have moved to the front burner for policy makers in the White House and Congress, along with health care.

Many corporations and individual states have been addressing energy use and climate impact for several years. The Obama administration has put world-class scientists Steven Chu and John Holdren in charge of the nation's energy and science policies. This bodes well for good decision making. The United States has already announced its intention to take a leadership role in the upcoming Copenhagen discussions, which are the follow-up to the earlier Kyoto Protocol on climate change. It also appears that China will move forward with its own greener policies; this is critical because that nation is now the world's largest emitter of greenhouse gases, including carbon dioxide.

Facing the Problem Head On

History clearly shows that economic transitions can be very painful. This is especially true when prior excesses must be corrected and when long-term structural changes affect the viability of some industries and business models. I don't mean to minimize this truth at all. The current transition will continue to be uncomfortable, but we will ultimately emerge on the other side. I believe that many capable policy makers in Washington have understood the depth and dimensions of the joint economic and financial market crises and have shown great wisdom—but not perfection—in the steps that have been taken as a result. The economy has not yet recovered, but it looks less bleak. Markets are not yet normal, but they're moving more normally. There is the recognition on both sides of the political aisle that greater attention and funding may be needed to kick-start certain activities, such as enhanced education and research and development (R&D) in energy. The most important thing about solving a problem is recognizing that you have it. The past couple of years have revealed many problems that were previously ignored, and we have begun to respond.

7

Paul McCulley

Paul McCulley is a managing director, generalist portfolio manager, and member of the investment committee at PIMCO, a global investment management firm co-founded by bond guru Bill Gross. Their clients range from universities to municipalities to pension funds to central banks. Paul is also in charge of PIMCO's short-term bond desk, leads its cyclical economic forums, and is the author of the monthly research publication *Global Central Bank Focus*. Prior to joining PIMCO in 1999, he was chief economist for the Americas at UBS Warburg. Paul's financial knowledge and ability to anticipate trends before they happen make him one of the most listened-to financial experts in the country.

The first and most important thing for people who are active in the markets—as well as "regular" citizens—to recognize is that the financial crisis has been an epoch-changing event. Although a number of elements of this change have occurred over the past couple of years—the subprime crisis, the credit crisis, massive deleveraging, and so forth—things really reached a new level after Lehman Brothers went to its watery death on September 15, 2008.

Every economy strikes a balance between the dual influences of the democratic process and the marketplace; or, as I like to put it, an economy is a weighted average of the invisible hand of the markets and the visible fist of governments. There is always tension between the invisible hand and the visible fist for a very simple reason: Capitalism is a cumulative voting process. The more dollars you have, the more votes you have; that's reflected by the simple fact that your boss goes to fancier restaurants than you do. That is a cumulative voting process, whereas democracy is, at its core, a socialist voting process: one person, one vote. So, there is inherent tension between the influences on capitalism and democracy, but they need each other.

The Need for Capitalism

A democracy needs capitalism to allocate resources based on a profit motive, because the government is not very good at allocating resources. Central planning has not stood the test of time, but the capitalist process of creative destruction has, and we've found that governments actually need the private market. Likewise, capitalism needs government for one simple reason: to help maintain the rule of law and property rights.

Capitalism cannot inherently define a credible rule of law, because again, it is a cumulative voting process. If you left it to the capitalist system to make up the rule of law, it would create a situation in which the quality of your justice is related to the money you have to buy that justice, a situation that is obviously not tenable or credible. So democracy's gift to capitalism is the rule of law, and the basic proposition is that no one is above the rule of law. That is why, periodically, we have seen people who were formally famous for their fancy suits with vertical pinstripes later having to do the "perp walk" wearing horizontal pinstripes. Such things reinforce the fact that nobody is above the rule of law.

Over the past 25 years, the invisible hand of the marketplace was in its ascendancy, and the visible fist of government was in retreat. So for a quarter century, we were actually tilting the weights more toward capitalism and less toward government. The catchwords for that phenomenon were *deregulation* and *globalization.* But the deregulated, globalized financial system took the invisible hand way too far and created a monstrous debt-deflation risk. Only the government can actually meet the forces of deflation with adequate counterforce of reflationary policies. It does so primarily by printing money, but also through its power to tax and borrow.

Essentially, this current crisis required that the government sector substitute itself for the broken invisible hand, which is truly a regime shift. That brings us to our current situation—one wherein capitalism is in retreat and government is in ascendancy—something that is a hugely important point for businesses, investors, and citizens. The 25-year bull market in capitalism has come to an ignominious end, and we have begun a new bull market in government.

The New Economy

Whether you like or dislike the ascendancy of government and retreat of markets is a philosophical issue. But as a factual matter, it's happening; and we must adjust our strategies to reflect the change in the relationship between the invisible hand of the visible fist. There will be slower potential economic growth, because deeper government involvement in the economy means we'll lose some of the dynamic productivity gains that we've achieved through the process of creative destruction. So first and foremost, these transformations mean that over the next 5 to 10 years, growth is not going to be as robust as it was during the 25 years of ascendancy of the invisible hand.

The second outcome is that we are going to have more regulation. The American people, through the democratic process, have espoused a "never again" mentality, which means that there will be strings attached to the bailouts that we, the people, have provided. Investors and companies will have to operate knowing that they are going to be living in a much more regulated economy than they had been. This also has a damping effect on economic growth.

The third outcome is that we are going to see a modest pullback in the globalization process. We are going to kill it, so I'm not worried about a repeat of past mistakes like a Smoot-Hawley Act of 2010.* But when governments have to step up to the plate to bail out broken markets, it tends to have a nationalistic flavor. This is obviously the case in the United States and in other countries around the globe as well.

If governments are going to put taxpayers' money at risk, they have to ensure that citizens are the predominant beneficiaries. This causes governments to act in a nationalistic fashion, because citizens are the ones who vote. So U.S. citizens, for example, will want to receive an outsized benefit from U.S. bailouts, which is inherently nationalistic.

---

* *Author's note:* Smoot-Hawley was officially known as the Tariff Act of 1930, which raised U.S. import duties on more than 20,000 imported goods to record rates. Although initially the act seemed to be a success because of a sharp increase in construction contracts, industrial production, and factory payrolls, global retaliation to the act led to the dismantling of global trade. In 1932, both Smoot and Hawley were defeated for reelection, which has been largely blamed on the controversial tariff.

Emerging Opportunities

Investors today face a handful of key issues, the biggest of which is that a more regulated economy with lower potential growth is going to have implications on what is considered a normalized stock price-to-earnings (P/E) multiple. Stocks will have a lower normalized P/E multiple, so I think investors have to think in terms of what it means to go for growth.

The growth that we will see on a global basis will be in emerging economies, which are likely going to accelerate efforts to build domestic consumption and move away from the mercantilist model. The mercantilist model required the U.S. consumers to shop till they dropped, but the problem is that that they have shopped, and now, dropped. Emerging economies will need to have more homespun growth, something that is happening in China now and beginning to happen in India and Brazil.

These changes in emerging markets won't come overnight, but as we look toward the next 10 years, developing countries will move directionally away from mercantilism and toward a model of domestic demand and increasing standards of living for workers. There should come a day when a guy who makes flat-screen TVs in China doesn't put one in a box and ship it to the United States, but rather puts it in the truck and takes it home to actually enjoy the fruits of his own labor. So I am enthusiastic on the structural secular theme with respect to emerging markets.

Investment Strategies

For asset allocation, investors will want to maintain lower equity concentrations in this "new normal" than they did in the old normal and, within the context of a reduced equity allocation, an even greater weight in emerging market equities. I have nothing particularly warm and fuzzy to say about government bonds in terms of fixed income, but I think bonds of quite heavily regulated private sector entities—especially the banking system—will offer relative value. We are moving more toward a utility model in the banking sector, as opposed to a Wild West model, which calls for a bigger allocation to high-grade corporate bonds than has historically been the case.

With respect to currencies, emerging markets offer significant opportunities. After having been beaten down during the height of the crisis, emerging market currencies are likely to rebound to reflect the greater growth potential inherent in that sector. So when I say people should have more exposure to emerging market equities and debt, they should have it broadly unhedged, meaning that they are taking non-dollar risk.

How PIMCO Is Thriving in the New Economy

As this crisis has been unfolding, PIMCO has navigated the marketplace with more alacrity than many of our competitors—because we were focused squarely on defense. We know from experience that it pays to perform well during a crisis because it helps to pick up market share.

But as the crisis continues on its course, we're moving cautiously toward opportunities to play offense. This doesn't necessarily mean taking big risks, but rather recognizing that we are moving toward a "new normal" in which our strategies will emphasize safe high-quality yield in the portfolio, as opposed to taking big bets on interest rates. Obviously, we had a 25-year bull market in Treasuries, and players that were long in the markets that did pretty well. But the story has changed since credit has been repriced from the nosebleed levels where it traded before the crisis. We now actually believe that many parts of the credit market are priced attractively relative to risk. On the equity side, there should also be a focus on yield amid a revival in sustainable dividends, and stocks that pay dividends are going to trade at a premium.

Being an Educator

There are obviously many lessons to be learned from the crisis, and it's as important as ever for an asset manager like PIMCO to play the role of trusted advisor to clients. We are not just doing an assignment for our clients; we are acting as their partner to help them work through what they need to do in this new world.

Among the fundamental issues in the United States right now is the need to rethink asset allocation. A lot of investors had moved to what is colloquially known as the Harvard or Yale model of portfolio construction, in which they maintained big allocations to illiquid and private instruments, such as private equity and hedge funds. The crisis has been particularly brutal for these types of illiquid instruments, which is one of the reasons so many colleges and universities with endowments that are highly illiquid or otherwise locked up have to issue taxable debt to get through the liquidity crunch. Clearly, these investors are going to view asset allocation differently going forward, and they're going to need help building portfolios that are not as susceptible to market crises.

Some of the greatest international shifts will come in terms of the approach investors take to the fixed-income market as opposed to the asset allocation paradigm itself. Prior to the crisis, the shadow banking system and structured finance industry had gone very global. Many investors outside the United States were buying various forms of structured credit that was stamped triple-A by Moody's and Standard and Poor's (S&P) 500 Stock Index, only to find out that it was not triple-A—and that they had bought a pig in a poke. So the nature of the shadow banking system and structured products was a critical issue that we have had to explain to international clients more often than domestic ones. We're also spending a great deal of time explaining the mechanics of the innovative new policies being carried out by the big three: the Treasury, the Fed, and the Federal Deposit Insurance Corporation (FDIC).

Thriving in the New Economy

Investors can thrive in the new economy, but they must accept three ideas to do so. The first is that you always need an adequate defense, especially against "tail risks" that, although infrequent, can be devastating to a portfolio. The second is that you have to embrace the fact that the world is changing and won't simply revert back to how it looked over the past few decades. The third is that you must accept that the offensive plays—the attractive investment returns—in this new world aren't going to be in the places that conventional wisdom has trained us to look for them.

8

Ron Baron

Whether the stock market is rising or falling, Baron Funds founder Ron Baron never loses sight of his long-term objective. With a time horizon of five years or often longer, Ron and his firm invest on behalf of their shareholders primarily in small and mid-sized growth companies, and the managements who run those businesses. The companies that attract Ron are financially strong, are well managed, and have prospects to become significantly larger. Ron and his firm use a bottom-up, intense company research strategy and try to invest in companies at what they believe are attractive prices.

When investing in growth companies, Ron uses a value-oriented purchase discipline. Short-term market fluctuations usually don't disturb him. If Baron Funds believes the fundamentals that justified an investment haven't changed, they will hold that investment and may even

(*continued*)

(continued)
buy more. This flies in the face of the response usually made by rule-based investors who sell when stock prices fall, assuming they must have made a mistake. Ron's long-term approach and focus require him to study the big picture: Just because a business is earning less money or even losing money for a short period does not mean that business's viability or long-term growth prospects are threatened. In most cases, Ron expects Baron Funds' current investments to recover the value they have lost between the fall of 2007 and the spring of 2009 during the next several years.

Ron Baron was smitten with stocks at age 13, when he invested his $1,000 bar mitzvah gifts and, in a rising market, immediately began to make money. Adding to his investments with earnings from shoveling snow, waiting tables, serving as a lifeguard, and selling ice cream—like so many students today—he helped pay his college tuition. Ron officially began his career in finance in 1970. He has witnessed numerous recessions and stock market "panics": the extended bear market of 1973 to 1974, the crash in 1987, the free fall after 9/11, and countless other market dysfunctions both in the United States and abroad. Ever the optimist, Ron says that no matter how bleak our economy's prospects may seem, our country and its economy have always recovered from distressing circumstances since its founding. He subscribes to Warren Buffett's philosophy that "pessimism is the friend of the investor" and to Ronald Reagan's motto that "America's best days lie ahead"; accordingly, he believes that "2009 offers investors the best opportunities of my lifetime." Although he began working in finance years ago, Ron's passion and excitement about investing still keep him up at night, especially now, with so many stocks at levels he finds unusually attractive.

Looking back, I think this crisis had many similarities to what happened following the Crash of 1929. I thought our government had learned the lessons of the 1930s and that tragic periods like that would be confined to history books. I didn't think we would see such things again: a financial chain reaction with continuing negative feedback that could cause an extraordinarily weak economy for an extended period. However, Lehman Brothers' bankruptcy on September 15, 2008, was the catalyst for just such a financial chain reaction. This is because Lehman Brothers' balance sheet was so large—just like AIG's—that virtually all the other large financial firms with whom it had done business were adversely affected when it failed.

When the stock market began to plunge day after day after September 15, real-time news coverage on television, the Internet, and newspapers brought these events into everyone's living room on a daily basis and in terrifying detail. It was like watching a catastrophe; it seemed surreal. The resulting fear in America and worldwide and the loss of confidence in our capacity to deal with crises caused stock markets here and globally to continue to fall. Investors, consumers, and businesspeople reacted, economies everywhere fell into a deep recession, and stocks fell further. It couldn't have been clearer to us what was happening when one corporation after another in which we had invested began to tell us they were cutting expenses, reducing employment, and cutting capital expenditures. That would clearly reduce consumer confidence and purchases, which would lead to even more business cost reductions, which would lead to even lower consumer confidence, and so on. It reminded me of the reported meeting early in the twentieth century between Henry Ford, the founder of Ford Motor Company, and Walter Reuther, the head of the United Auto Workers union, in one of Ford's new plants. "Do you see all those workers, Mr. Reuther? Some day all their jobs will be done by machines," Ford told Reuther. "Just who do you expect to buy your cars then, Mr. Ford?" Reuther replied. When businesses cut jobs, there are obviously fewer customers for their products. This is an immutable rule.

The situation with Lehman Brothers brought to mind Warren Buffett's comments regarding the propensity for one to rely upon someone else's promise: that the promise is no better than the ability and desire of the person making it to fulfill it. Lehman Brothers had made commercial promises to many upon which they relied to establish other commercial and contractual commitments. Many of those to whom Lehman Brothers had made these promises—promises it would now be unable to fulfill—and those counterparties could be greatly affected. But by how much? No one seemed to know. Lehman Brothers was so large. It was difficult to understand how the government could allow it to fail. But, for some reason, it did.

After Lehman Brothers' failure, it became clear how dangerously leveraged our economy had become, and how leveraging had been an important driver of our growth over the past 30 years. Borrowing allowed people to buy things they could not have bought otherwise; it made assets more valuable than they ever might have been. This trend could have ended at any time, even 5 or 10 years ago. Indebtedness in our economy increased from about 170 percent of the gross domestic product (GDP) in 1982 to 350 percent of the GDP in 2009. We simply could not support that indebtedness if either interest rates increased or the economy faltered.

Learning from Mistakes

Everyone makes mistakes when circumstances change rapidly, so we of course made some during the past 18 months. How did we react? On the margin, we tried to make the portfolios we managed more resistant to the Great Recession of 2009. We reduced our investments in businesses that used leverage or required access to capital markets. We reduced our investments in businesses that provide consumers with nonessential products and services. We increased our investments in education, health care, and infrastructure and were even more opportunistic than usual when purchasing investments. Despite the recession, at year-end 2008, we expected more than half the companies in which we had invested to have higher earnings in 2009 than they did in 2008. We have also recognized losses that we could use to shelter future investment earnings.

No Sleep

I speak with our employees; I speak with executives of companies in which we invest; and, I speak with my family and with my friends. My best friends are individuals with whom I've been close nearly my entire life. One of my best friends, Jack, is a doctor who now lives in Palo Alto. We've been friends since I was 11 or 12 years old. A few months ago, he said to me, "Ronnie, I have been investing with you for 30 years. Because of that, I am fine and have a lot of money; but after this year about half as much as I had. I could easily live on that; but I just can't live on nothing." Jack is one of the most laid-back people I know, but he wasn't sleeping well. I told him that although I am rarely upset by market movements and economic forecasts, there were times when I also didn't sleep well. My wife and my closest colleagues, both of whom are usually fairly hard to upset, have also had a difficult time sleeping. Regardless, during most of this period I have been in very good spirits and have viewed events as providing us with what I have called the best investment opportunities of my lifetime.

Looking for Leadership

After Lehman Brothers collapsed, I told our researchers that our country was going to emerge from this difficult period and that it was more important than ever to focus on research instead of worrying about what is unpredictable. We research businesses. We analyze companies and study people. We try to find people with whom we want to invest, and who we think are smart, hard-working, and honest, and we bet on them. Find great businesses with really big opportunities and people who can make those businesses become a lot larger. It doesn't matter how great the opportunity is; unless you find someone who is going to realize that opportunity for the business, it's not going to happen. There couldn't be a better time to do research, I told our staff, than when there is so much turmoil and uncertainty—and so many are concerned with losing their jobs that they're not doing their jobs. If we can't find great investment ideas now, I remarked, we'll never be able to find great investment ideas.

Realizing Opportunities

We have been investing in education companies since 1990. The idea when we started investing in for-profit colleges 19 years ago was that they awarded you the same accredited degree that you would receive when you went to a state college or the top private colleges and universities. Students could attend for-profit colleges for less than it would cost to go to a state college. Not only was it less expensive, but it was easier to gain admission.

Two examples of company leadership that attracted us were DeVry's Ron Taylor and Strayer Education's Rob Silberman. The market value of DeVry in 1990, when we began to invest in that business, was about $100 million. It has since grown more than thirty-fold, to more than $3 billion. DeVry was even selected to replace General Motors Corporation in the S&P 500 Stock Index! DeVry's Ron Taylor and Strayer Education's Rob Silberman care about whether their students graduate and can get jobs when they do, earning twice as much as they could before they attended those colleges. Neither executive was attempting to maximize their enrollments and short-term profits; they were simply trying to make sure their students were receiving a high-quality education. Many of DeVry's students were the first in their families to attend college. Often the children of immigrants or minorities who were the product of an inadequate high school education, they were unlikely to be successful. DeVry provided them with courses in remedial reading, English as a first language, and math skills that should have been taught in high school or maybe even grammar school. They made sure that their students would actually have the skills they needed to succeed in college. Strayer requires that its students take laboratory and science courses to make certain they receive a well-rounded education. Although some of these programs were not profitable, they gave students tools to be successful both in college and upon graduation.

Steve Wynn is a CEO with whom I have been investing since 1980. I was introduced to Steve by Jay Pritzker, the founder of Global Hyatt Corporation. "Steve Wynn? What kind of name is that for a guy in casinos? Is he a comic strip character?" I wanted to know. Jay said, "No. No, this is a guy you have to meet. He's the best operator in his industry." Well, I met Steve in 1980 and have been investing with him since. We invested about $135 million in 2001 in Wynn Resorts, have received perhaps $80 million in dividends and had earned more than $1 billion before we gave up about 35 percent of that amount since November 2007.

Why do we think Steve is a great manager? One of Baron Funds' outside directors, Alex Yemenidjian, is a mutual friend of Steve's and mine. As someone who previously worked for Kirk Kerkorian as chairman of MGM Grand, the casino hotel business, and MGM Studios, Alex claims the only guy who really gets it right in Las Vegas is Steve Wynn. That is because Steve wants to be certain that when his guests visit his hotels, they are treated well and want to return. Wynn Las Vegas is different than other properties, Alex explains, because when you stay there, you feel like you are staying at a country inn run by its proprietor who lives upstairs. Steve does indeed live there, knows all the people who work for him, and ensures that they provide the services he would expect to provide to friends and family guests coming to visit him.

An example of this was back in the 1970s, a wealthy individual from Japan visited Steve's Atlantic City casino hotel and requested a line of credit, which Steve approved. They gave that individual a $10 or $15 million credit line, which, in the 1970s, was an extraordinary amount of money. It was also a lot of money to lose if the customer won a substantial amount of money. Well, the individual won $10 million that weekend. When Steve's hotel guest arrived home in Tokyo, there was a Rolls-Royce in his driveway, wrapped in a pink ribbon with a note from Steve attached. "Thank you very much for visiting our casino. We look forward to serving you again." Well, that person returned to Steve's Golden Nugget a couple of weeks later. He lost all those winnings and an additional $15 million.

Steve knows that is the way you treat people if you want them to always stay in your hotel, and he is highly regarded in his community. He takes good care of his employees, who in return take good care of his customers. If you are not concerned about your reputation in your community, you won't attract great employees who will treat your customers well. And it doesn't really matter how much your earnings increase in any given quarter; you are ultimately going to fail. Steve is the perfect example of someone who has the vision to run a successful hospitality business.

Thriving Strategies

Most people run businesses to maximize earnings and profits in the short term. The executives with whom we prefer to invest think about the long term. They put money into their businesses even when it could potentially endanger profitability in the short term. Their objective is to invest in order to create competitive advantage for their business so that it can become much larger in the long term.

Our office is very welcoming. Why have we made the effort to make it so? It's because we believe that if you give someone light, pretty space, and a view, they will be happier; they will feel better; they will act positively; and they will become friendly with one another. They will be excited about their jobs and proud to have their children and spouses visit on a weekend to see where they work. Our fellow employees' families and parents come by all the time. One of the results of having such a pleasant work environment is the tendency to show respect for your fellow workers. They are better employees. They work harder, and they treat our customers, the shareholders of our mutual funds, better. Our reputation in the community is solid. As a result, we are able to hire great employees; they treat our customers well, and the owners of our family business are doing well. If you do not put effort into those other things, you will fail. A good manager is someone who thinks about all of these aspects of business, and that's what we're looking for. That's the sort of personality that you must have; rather than being short-term oriented, you must look at the long term.

For years, our country has not had a long-term plan. The chief executive of Singapore is 80 years old. He has a 100-year plan! New York City had never had a plan. Michael Bloomberg was elected Mayor and the city now has a 35-year plan. I read in the newspaper this week that the head of the New York City teachers union had been concerned about Bloomberg's control over education in New York City. But, according to this individual, since Bloomberg wrested control over our city's schools, look what has happened to our city's student population. Student math test scores in New York City schools have skyrocketed. So have other metrics measuring education outcomes. Mayor Bloomberg's long-term plan is to make people in New York healthier, to make it impossible to smoke in restaurants, to tax carbonated soda, to keep you from drinking diet sodas because they are unhealthy. Bloomberg wants to have healthier people, trimmer people, and no diabetes. In addition to benefitting our populace directly, our health care bill will be less. Mayor Bloomberg has a plan.

President Obama also has a plan. You might not agree with all parts of it, but he has one; he has a vision for where he wants to take our country. He wants to make our country different than it has been. We have been using too much carbon energy for a long time. It has become too expensive to continue to do so. We have been sending our money overseas to pay for energy, giving foreigners a claim on our assets. This has been hurting our dollar and is allowing foreigners to buy our assets on the cheap. By selling our assets cheaply, we have been damaging our economy; we have been making our country less safe by relying on nations who are not our friends to provide us with what is necessary to operate our economy. Along the way, we have been damaging our environment.

President Obama is trying to make America more efficient in its use of energy. He's going to make our economy less leveraged; he's going to make our financial institutions stronger. Right now, we have banks that want to pay back their Troubled Asset Relief Program (TARP) money. But the government has responded, "Not so fast." They won't permit them to pay it back until they can show the government that they're solvent and can raise equity money from public investors. Why is the President doing this? To make sure that these companies really are solvent and that they are not going to cause a repeat of the financial crisis we are now in the process of resolving. This is great, what our government is doing.

Obama Administration Investing

There is a terrific opportunity in wind power, which is produced on the great plains of America, in the middle of the country. The users of wind power are the guys who live on the coasts. But how do you get the energy there? You need transmission. We have an investment in ITC Holdings, the largest, and only independent, publicly owned, electricity transmission company. It was a spin out from Detroit Edison.

Get Excited

When the market falls as much as it has recently, you can throw a dart and virtually anything you hit is going to make you money in the short term. The trick is to find something that is not going to go up just in the short term. In fact, since the U.S. market bottomed in early March 2009, stocks of lower-quality businesses have increased in price more than those of higher-quality businesses. This is because low-quality, highly leveraged businesses were left for dead by investors—and they did not die. But what are the opportunities for those companies for the long term? There is investment opportunity for the long term in education, making sure that people can afford to be educated and make our nation more productive and more competitive in the world.

Health care is another big investment opportunity. We recently visited genetic testing company Gen-Probe in California; they told us about their new prostate cancer test called PCA 3 (prostate cancer gene 3). Instead of a prostate-specific antigen (PSA) culture test, which takes two or three weeks to obtain results with only okay accuracy (you get a lot of false-positive and false-negative results), Gen-Probe's genetic test will give you results in two or three hours—and it is 99 percent accurate. I inquired as to why they still do a PSA test if it is inaccurate, is expensive, and takes three weeks versus three hours to get results. I was told the reason is that we have an infrastructure in America that makes a great deal of money from PSA tests—tests that are inaccurate, expensive, and obsolete. This scientist explained to us that many believe almost one-third of the amount of money spent on medical care in our country is wasted.

Investing Criteria

We at Baron Funds are plain-vanilla investors who employ a very simple strategy: find a business that can double in size in four or five years by providing an important service that others cannot easily provide to a clientele who could not otherwise obtain that service at an attractive price. We are trying to find businesses that are or can become very profitable, operated by individuals we like. It's as simple as that.

We tell our clients that we are betting on someone.

We are betting on the people who run businesses with big opportunities to work hard to make their businesses become larger. People understand that, and they say okay, I got it. That sounds reasonable to me. This takes me back to high school. When you are young, you know who the smartest kid in your class is; you know whom you like the best. You know who you think is honest. And that's all this is. This business is about betting on people, about betting on people who have the long-term vision and are willing to sacrifice short-term profits to make their business impregnable over the long term. That's what this is all about.

9

Ken Langone

No one embodies or embraces the entrepreneurial spirit more than Ken Langone. Cofounder of The Home Depot and chairman and CEO of Invemed Associates, as well as a former New York Stock Exchange (NYSE) Board member, Ken is an inspiration to many students who want to succeed. To help pay for his tuition at Bucknell University, Ken worked as a caddie, ditch digger, and a butcher's assistant. Majoring in economics and political science, Ken finished in three and a half years. He then went to NYU, working full-time during the day at Equitable Life Assurance Company and attending courses at night. The part-time evening program is still proudly called the "Langone Program."

Ken has decades of experience bringing companies public. The first deal of his career was the IPO launch of Ross Perot's company Electronic Data Systems, and then of

(continued)

(*continued*)
course, his most prominent deal: The Home Depot. Ken's pulse on the economy spans not only from his Invemed investments but also from his board seats of Yum! Brands and Unified. Ken's investment bank, Invemed Associates, either takes minority stakes in small cap companies, invests in buyouts, or start-up companies. The key to Ken's success, and you'll read about it in a few minutes, is that Invemed does not use leverage in making any of its investments. Ken is a long-term investor, usually holding companies for 5 to 10 years in the firm's portfolio.

Ken's entrepreneurial experience and the challenges he has faced and conquered have made him who he is today. As I sat in his office waiting to start the interview, I was looking at the photos on his long side table. And among the photos there was one in particular that jumped out to me: a small frame that looked like a dartboard with a photo of Eliot Spitzer in it. Ken has chosen to take the high road when it comes to his battle with the disgraced "Luv Gov" and former New York Attorney General who unsuccessfully prosecuted him for the controversial pay package of former NYSE chief Dick Grasso.

Ken is very passionate about what he does, and you can hear it in his words. He never loses sight of his objective, and his criteria and approach to business are what investors gravitate toward.

Bear Stearns was really the contagion that had gone from the firm's hedge funds and spread its way to other firms throughout the entire system. When Bear Stearns' hedge funds hit the wall in the summer of 2007, it was clear one of the reasons they were having problems was that the people managing those funds did not fully understand the degree of risk in what they were buying. For whatever reason these people were in these securities—maybe they were depending on ratings or they thought they knew what they were doing or they thought they could make a lot of money—they ended up being financially exposed beyond what I think their calculations indicated.

Whether it was structured investment vehicles (SIVs), credit default swaps, or collateral debt obligations, it didn't matter. There were layers upon layers of leverage being added to a system, which meant that when it froze up, you were in trouble. So we fast-forward to Bear Stearns' demise, or should I say its fire sale, to J.P. Morgan. By then, the forest fire was raging. Morgan Stanley, Goldman Sachs, Merrill Lynch—they all went right down. It was clear that much of the activity of the past five or six years was in financial instruments where the risks were far greater. The collateral risk, the interlinked risk between one firm and another firm, was profound. I have never trafficked in that kind of paper. I never understood it. I don't buy what I don't understand.

At the time, I said to myself, "Something bad is happening right now." The instruments themselves created a problem. Nobody understood how they worked. But it was made a far more profound problem by the sheer size of the total amount of this outstanding paper. It was staggering. And it'd gone beyond America's shores. It had gone to communities in Scandinavian countries that were getting racked by values that were almost evaporating. It became a guessing game of who would survive and who would not.

From the time Bear Stearns was sold, throughout the entire next six months until Lehman Brothers was allowed to go bankrupt, it was clear that the rangers were looking for a way to contain this forest fire. The lesson we all got from the depression was that a lack of liquidity only exacerbates the problem. So to the government's credit, it inundated the markets—I mean swamped the markets, flaunted them, with cash of various sizes and ways of getting the money in. For example, it had the Troubled Asset Relief Program (TARP) money, then it had the Term Asset-Backed Securities

Loan Facility (TALF) money, and before the TARP money, it was going to loan money to the banks to make loans, which I found a bit contradictory because that's what got us in trouble. Too many people were borrowing money that they couldn't pay back.

Economic Reality

As the economy began to respond to this financial crisis, people reacted by pulling their horns in. General Motors and Ford were on the edge. Ford is a different story. I push Ford over to the side because Ford borrowed a lot of money—a lot of older money—and still has it. When sales of automobiles tanked, dropping from $12 million a year to $11 million, then to $10 million, and now it looks like $9.5 million, GM's and Chrylser's market shares eroded. They both ended up needing to be put into bankruptcy, but not before the government gave them significant sums of money in December 2008. I said it then and will say it again now: There was a strong feeling that Chrysler and General Motors should have been allowed to go bankrupt in December 2008. But the government gave them something like $60 or $80 billion. Will the government ever get it back? Who knows. In order for General Motors to be worth $50 billion, and assuming the 500 million shares of stock outstanding was there and not wiped out in bankruptcy, the stock would have to go to $100 a share. I don't see it in the cards.

So we have put ourselves in a position where we have dissipated enormous pools of assets; we have exchanged them for assets such as homes and cars that have had a significant erosion in value. How do you deal with that? I read an article that stated that Detroit is trying to get people to consolidate, live on blocks, so that they can at least offer some degree of municipal services, such as refuse collection, lighting, fire, police—the whole bit. But if you have one block that has 3 homes on it, and you have another block that has 40 homes but only 2 or 3 are occupied, it doesn't make sense to scatter out. So I think the next thing I am concerned about is municipalities that are going to wake up and say we can't provide services because we don't have the money. They haven't got the tax base. Worse, the population is sparse, and what do you do? California has serious problems. Are we going to ask our federal government to bail out the municipalities in California? Or the municipalities in New York? I hope not. I hope we do not get to that point. The president said properly in early June 2009 that we do not have any more money. At least we understand that if we print any more money, we are almost guaranteeing the problems that I am concerned about.

So none of us alive, none of us, and I am going to be 74, have seen anything like this. It is all new. We are looking at an environment where huge sums of paper called money are flooding the system. That was a necessary condition for activity in September 2008. The Fed is monetizing the federal government's debt. That typically leads to inflation. All of us who remember the 1970s remember stagflation. We had an economy that was stagnant and prices that were going through the roof, not because of supply and demand but because of this enormous flood of cash.

When I read in the paper that the government is going to start allowing some of the financial institutions to repay the TARP money, I found that very constructive. But that doesn't take away from the fact that we have a fundamental underlying problem, which is this surge of cash coming. And I don't know how we can have a robust economy with our two biggest industries—housing and autos—in the tank.

Now maybe I am wrong, but I do not see the automobile industry really perking up for a couple of years. I think you look at supply and demand of homes, and we probably have a three-year window. Yet through it all, I am optimistic. The first step to solving a problem is to acknowledge that you have a problem. We are doing that. The second step is to determine what technique to use to address the problem. What can I do to try to solve the problem? I am very concerned that we have gone beyond reasonable limits in funding all these different institutions. I am not sure I agree with this notion. I know we had to do it to prevent a depression. But I am still concerned about it.

New Economy Strategy

Through this entire crisis, starting at the onset all the way through the advance phase in September, I made sure Invemed Associates stayed highly liquid. We made sure our credit and our cash had jumped big time. It stayed at that level because we have significant investments, either mine or the firm's, and if there was an investment opportunity we would have a chance to participate. But more importantly, we made certain that we were not dependent on the banks for whatever capital means we had.

Hopefully the wickedness of this entire period is going to make it easier for people to be mindful of the fact that leverage needs to have limitations. The guy who rents you money expects to get his money. We are now learning how much damage has been done. It is like a person in a head-on collision—the recovery is going to take longer than he thinks. Our eyes are now wide open. I am not sure I agree with this surge of paper. I am not sure I would not say, "Wait a minute, the idea is not to get this thing back up where it was. The idea is to sort of get it back up on a sound footing, and then go from there." I would feel a lot better about that.

Debt has its place. That said, I hope all of us understand the risks of excess leverage, and of excess borrowing. When you live in such a way that your survival depends on the sun shining each and every day, you are living on the edge of a very unrealistic expectation.

Investing Criteria

I am always looking for opportunities. One person's pain is another person's pleasure. We are looking for companies with very strong balance sheets, with good and protectable cash flows. Companies whose management has demonstrated the willingness or the desire to have some form of shareholder reward—hopefully dividends, but maybe buybacks. We are looking for companies that can sustain themselves and their capital needs. Because I think now we all know that the banks have been badly wounded.

Many of them are now so-called penny stocks. But that's okay. I am looking for companies with balance sheets that are so strong that the cash they have is close to or greater than the price of the stock. One of the companies we invest in is called SourceForge. That is the old VA Linux. Then there's the textile company called Unified, for which I am a member of the board. I am hopeful that we will be able to get something done there. We certainly have a good management team in place at Unified. Financially, we have our back to the wall; we have some significant debt, but the cash flow is good. We are keeping the facilities in tip-top shape. Regrettably, the textile industry is moving offshore—not entirely, but a significant percentage that impacts it. Other sectors that I keep an eye on are education and medical technology, or biotech devices. I also look at health care stocks in general and some retail companies. I always have my eyes open for things. I have more time now to contemplate an investment than I did before because the markets are not moving that quickly.

10

Peter Cohen

Peter Cohen, founder of the $7.5 billion alternative asset management company Ramius, is yet another great economic mind. Peter was also the former chairman and chief executive of Shearson Lehman Brothers from 1983 to 1999 and has served on many boards of directors, including the New York Stock Exchange, L-3 Communications Holdings, American Express, Olivetti SpA, and Telecom SpA.

Despite the challenges that still lie ahead in the financial services industry, Peter's strategies have enabled his company to grow where others are clawing their way to survive. In June 2009, Ramius announced its purchase of investment boutique firm Cowen Group in a "reverse

(*continued*)

(*continued*)
merger,'' referred to as such because Ramius exchanged a substantial portion of its assets and liabilities for a 71 percent controlling stake in the newly combined company. This $195 million deal opened a new door for Peter and provided access to the public markets and the ability to forge a path in the beaten-down investment banking sector. Peter claims that this deal represents what the future of Wall Street will look like.

The origins of this crisis go back a good many years before the September 2008 meltdown. It was apparent that access to credit was spinning out of control, leverage in the global system was irresponsibly excessive, and companies were being bought in private equity transactions at unprecedented valuations financed with an unheard-of amount of leverage. We would look at the situation and say, we can't work it; it can't be done—yet it continued. We saw the first real cracks in February 2007, with the residential mortgage-backed securities (RMBS) market. In fairness, most people—ourselves included—believed that the problem was principally isolated to subprime mortgages, where there had been tremendous abuse that bordered on illegality. We believed prime jumbo and conforming mortgages were probably okay. As much as we read about how global leverage was going to overwhelm the system, it kept growing. We're paid to manage money and not to be totally out of the markets, even though one could look back and say, "Geez, maybe we should have turned everything into cash."

We do a lot of different things for our clients. In addition to a number of liquid market strategies, we buy real estate, we make loans on real estate, invest in oil and gas businesses, conduct private placements in public companies, and execute some small private equity deals—but we do them without leverage. We thought that although we weren't totally immune from problems, we were somewhat safely on the fringe of the leverage mania. And when the problem came home to roost, although it might sting, it wasn't going to be the awful bite that it turned out to be for everybody's portfolios, including ours.

Anticipating the Crisis

By and large, and with rare exception, everybody underestimated the severity of what was really taking place. We had informal conversations at the New York Federal Reserve Bank. We talked to them about the leverage; weren't they worried about it? In particular, weren't they worried about some of the securities firms? Having run a big security firm myself, the idea of 30, 40, or 50 times leverage—and what they were leveraged against—was attention-getting. It seemed that it was only a matter of time until the issue became a problem.

We visited the Fed in December 2007 and asked if they were thinking about making liquidity available to securities firms when and if they needed it. They informed us that they didn't see it as a likely scenario, stating that the Fed had not opened the discount window to securities firms since the Depression and it wasn't likely to happen again. Then, all of a sudden—Bear Stearns is on their doorstep on the verge of imploding. Even then, we thought that the problem was primarily specific to Bear Stearns. We didn't think it was systemic of the entire industry yet, because Bear Stearns was the leading mortgage securitization firm. It seemed natural that since mortgages were now starting to unravel, if there is going to be a problem, they were the ones who were going to have it. So the Bear Stearns problem erupts but is resolved through a Fed facility and merger with J.P. Morgan. We were actually somewhat relieved, because we thought the regulators now understood the problem and, having dealt with Bear Stearns, would handle any new problems as well. In fact, everyone took a certain amount of solace from their behavior when they saved Bear Stearns. We believed they did understand the situation that was unfolding in Washington. They opened the discount window. The world re-normalized pretty quickly by the spring of 2008.

House in Order

From an investment point of view, we were actually in good shape through August 2008. Our performance was up or even in everything we did, even though there was increasing volatility, especially in July. When Lehman Brothers began to take the spotlight, we assumed that the Fed—having exhibited a high degree of prudence about Bear Stearns—would reach the same conclusion about Lehman Brothers, if necessary.

After Bear Stearns, we attempted to more deeply understand how everybody with whom we did business was funded. We wanted to be comfortable in our interactions with Lehman Brothers, Goldman Sachs, or anyone else. We went through a very exhaustive process, with Lehman Brothers especially, to try to understand their entire liquidity funding strategy. We concluded that they had termed out all of their long-term debt and had substantial liquidity and excess collateral they could take to the Fed. Coupled with the idea that the Fed was informed enough to understand the implications of a failure, we concluded that Lehman Brothers would probably be okay.

We decreased our exposure to Lehman Brothers from being one of our larger prime brokers to being a third prime broker behind Goldman Sachs and Morgan Stanley. In our conversations with people at the Fed, we stated that letting Lehman Brothers fail would be catastrophic; the systemic risk was too high. We told them that we hoped they understood the complexity of the plumbing in the industry that connected the financial system. It wasn't until later that week that we started to believe the regulators could potentially make a mistake by letting the firm go, that they really didn't understand what was going to happen. The weekend before Lehman Brothers' failure, we kept reiterating to those we knew at the Fed—whomever we could get to—not to let this happen; we did not believe they understood how bad it would get.

The truth about what happened is not clear to me; I'm not sure anyone's really ever going to know except the people involved. I don't think there was any conspiracy by the rest of Wall Street to see Lehman Brothers fail. I don't know if Hank Paulson had any kind of problem with Dick Fuld, but even if he did, he's too smart to make a decision based on personal feelings. It was just a lapse of judgment on the part of the decision makers, whoever they were. They simply didn't understand the risks and somehow felt the moral hazard issue to which everyone kept referring was so important that they would let somebody fail, and deal with the consequences afterward.

It was a horrific mistake. Although the financial fallout would have still been substantial even if Lehman Brothers had been saved, it wouldn't have happened with the speed and magnitude it did. The situation caught the regulators completely unaware, because they seemed panicked after the market's reaction. The Lehman Brothers' failure happened on a Monday; on Tuesday, the Fed and Treasury suddenly had AIG on their plate. They knew they had to save AIG, but at the same time, they made the statement that they had no legal authority to save Lehman Brothers. The Fed and Treasury bailed out AIG the next day. In fact, by Tuesday, they were lending money to Lehman Brothers against collateral, which they could have done on Monday. Then on Wednesday, the market went into a meltdown. On Thursday the Fed and Treasury announced the Troubled Asset Relief Program (TARP), which was invented overnight. No one had any idea how it would work; it was clear it had not previously been on the drawing board.

All about Leverage

It started to become clear to everybody fairly quickly that this wasn't just a subprime problem anymore. It was really a systemic leverage problem across the entire financial system. As people started digging more deeply, it was apparent that both the U.S. and European banks had significant problems. It went way beyond subprime for U.S. banks. They not only had all the commercial mortgages that were held on balance sheet, but also had all the securitized commercial mortgages, credit card receivables, home equity loans, and more. These were big problems and on top of them was the Madoff event, which fractured everybody's confidence. It spurred a complete meltdown of confidence in the system, which was reflected in the markets.

After Christmas 2008, I returned to work assuming that January and February were just going to be more of the same. We were not out of the woods, although everybody thought with 2008 behind us and 2009 being a new year, we were all going to make it back. But I didn't believe that. The equity markets had two difficult months at the beginning of 2009, but a tremendous bounce beginning in March. President Obama has done a very good job of trying to talk the economy and confidence up. His actions, along with the government pouring money into one thing after another, took the "crisis tone" out of the country and the financial markets.

Analyzing the Situation and Creating Opportunity

As we were going through this, we asked ourselves, "What does this all mean?" We concluded that life as everyone knew it was over in this country both in our personal and business lives—at least for a long time to come. People were going to start saving money again; they were going to be more frugal. The general sentiment was that we were returning to a 1950s to 1960s value system; America was going to live differently. The credit markets became totally dysfunctional in the middle of this, unlike anything that's ever happened in the past. We saw that as an opportunity, however, because the lack of credit would separate the winners and losers. For example, we have a list of criteria we use when looking for investments. We consider the yields of investment-grade, high-quality companies that have good businesses—with good cash flow, even in a severe recession; liquidity on their balance sheets; access to capital; and access to credit based on committed but undrawn backup lines. Short-duration yields of companies were selling at much higher yields than the long-dated paper of the same company. So we made a decision to start shifting our assets away from everything that we could and into credit. We have shifted one-third of our assets into credit. Going forward from here, given the rally, equities will be difficult. The likelihood is that equities will decline again before all of this is over.

Where to Put Your Money

One of the few places you can safely put your money and get a yield is in reasonably short-dated corporate credits of high quality. Two-year maturities are short-term securities, so instead of getting a half percent return, you are going to get 4 or 5 percent.* There are one-offs where you get paid more, and some opportunities that may arise where you can make a 7 or 8 percent return with a high degree of comfort. We have acted accordingly and continue to move in that direction.

It is also a good idea to own some gold. I believe that gold is artificially suppressed by central banks, because if gold were $2,000

---

* *Author's note:* Short-term securities are securities that range from one to four years. These securities are more liquid. They can be bonds, corporation notes, commercial paper, municipal notes, and banker's acceptances, which are also known as cashier's checks. These securities can be turned into cash at the original purchasing price or better on the open market. Investors can also leave the security to mature and then reinvest into another short-term maturity.

per ounce, the world would be in panic and confidence in financial assets challenged. But one day, gold could just spike, and that would shake the financial foundation of the world.

We have also become much more proactive in our macro-trading activities. There is a difference of opinion internally as to whether the bigger problem is deflation or inflation. At the end of the day, inflation becomes a bigger problem, although the timing is uncertain. Whether it's next week or two years from now, it's coming; the government can't print money and issue debt the way it is without creating enormous impetus for inflation. And it's going to happen worldwide, because everybody is doing the same thing. Even China, with all of its good news and proactive stimulus programs, has serious problems. Japan has serious problems. Korea has serious problems. Europe has terrible problems. So the printing presses are rolling. Central banks and governments desperately want to avoid the world falling into a deflationary trap, which is really hard to fix. This is where there's pressure in our current environment, because people do not want to spend money. They're saving money. All you have to do is go up and down Lexington Avenue or Madison Avenue and you see this. You travel to Europe, and no Americans are around. Airline traffic is contracting, and retail sales are weak, except at the very low end. But the government did what it had to do to avert a financial catastrophe.

New Age in Business

The notion that the Fed will know exactly when to pull back this liquidity in time to stop inflation is a difficult one—because nobody knows. We're experiencing a period of government intervention in business and the markets. The more you raise taxes and the more you take purchasing power out of the economy, the more people save, because they are afraid. We are a consumer-driven economy. If the consumer doesn't spend, this economy can't grow. Marry that to what is happening on the state level, where every state's budget is totally unbalanced and state revenues are collapsing. Their budget deficits are swelling. So you think the worst is behind us? No, it is not. Who is going to bail out the states, and how much is that going to cost? The public pension funds systems, which millions of people rely on to live, are underfunded as well.

You can go on and on with the amount of wealth destruction that took place, and with no yields in the marketplace. Corporate pensions are facing the same obstacles; these are two substantial new problems. They got so battered last year—as did endowments, charities, and insurance companies—that it's questionable as to how they are going to meet their obligations. So the real question is are the states going to raise taxes and take more purchasing power out of the system so they can par down their deficits? Less purchasing power means no economic recovery. We are in a terrible trap, and the government has no choice but to print money and lend. The reckoning is upon us. The quality of life in this country has to decrease. The next generations are not going to have the opportunities, in my opinion, that mine had.

Protecting Wealth

The focus is no longer on making money. It's all about not losing it, and protecting wealth. If inflation returns, you do not want to own debt; you want to be a debtor. That's why we keep durations short. But for the over-leveraged consumer, saving as much as possible and paying down debt is of paramount importance. This is hard to do, because wages are declining, working hours are decreasing, and two-person household incomes are becoming one-person incomes. Unemployment continues to rise, and quality of life in the United States is decreasing; and you have to think really carefully about what to do with money and where to put money.

At the same time, there are flaring geopolitical issues. Is Korea a problem? Who knows. Is Iran a problem? Who knows. Is Israel going to stand by and let Iran develop a nuclear weapon? I doubt it. The European Central Bank is worried about inflation, so they're holding rates higher than maybe they should—which is good for their savers in a way, but bad for their system because there's not enough liquidity flowing through Europe. The American Century was the 1900s, and it's over. This century will belong to Asia. They had been waiting for years for this to come, and it's here. They will have plenty of problems, but their people are going to be much better at handling them than we are.

Leading by Example

Our business is an institutional business. We have a limited number of individual retail-type accounts. Since December 2008, I've been inundated with people who tell me: "I don't know what to do with my money." "I can't take half a percent in treasuries." "I've lost so much money. What do I do?" They ask me what I am doing. I tell them I don't own any stocks; I own gold, and I own a lot of corporate debt, a lot of short-dated corporate debt. I'm just trying to protect my capital and get a decent yield on my money while I wait for the world to sort itself out. And all of a sudden they say, "Fine—do that for me." I've received a substantial amount of money from friends who just want safety with some yield.

The fact is that we all need to adjust our lifestyles. We are preaching this advice to all our young people. Don't expect to make the kind of money you made before, because it's not going to be there. Raising money institutionally is almost impossible right now, except for credit strategies. They don't want to hear about private equity. They don't want to hear about real estate. They don't want to hear about exotic strategies. They want their money back, and they don't want to be in a fund. They want to be in a separate account, an account that allows them to see their money and know it belongs to them. And they want to do all this without paying the old kind of fees. That's what's happening now.

Characterizing the New Economy

The new economy is one of very modest growth, if any, for quite a while. We are all going to be leading more frugal lives. Everyone is rethinking everything they do. People are going to eat at more basic kinds of restaurants. It won't be the watch du jour. If Bernie Madoff paid $4,000 for a pair of pants, that may be the last pair of pants that were sold at that price. Who needs to buy a new car every two or three years? Buy a car every four years. Or buy a used car with a factory warranty on it. Cars don't wear out anymore. And how many suits does anyone really need? How many shirts does anyone have to have? How many of anything does anyone need? We were seduced into buying to excess through advertising and peer pressure. It's not a natural lifestyle and doesn't exist in most other places.

We're facing a much less consumer-oriented society. People are going to return to more core values about life. It's also going to be hard, because the jobs are not here anymore. That's why you have a record number of applicants for college, law school, and medical school. I just hope that people see engineering as a career path so that we get people going back to start inventing and manufacturing things again in this country.

Strategies to Thrive in the New Economy

There will be a reshaping of the financial industry in the new economy. The big investment banks are either part of a bank, or they've become a bank like Goldman Sachs and Morgan Stanley. They're large, they're somewhat unwieldy, they have a lot of red tape, and people would rather be somewhere perhaps smaller. So there is going to be a reemergence of smaller, broad-based, middle-tier firms that will be in the underwriting business, the advisory business, the sales and trading business, and the investment management business, which is where all these firms originally started. Our firm has never been in the underwriting business. We've never been in the corporate advisory business, and sales and trading were never part of our business. We were investors. We will continue to be investors, but we will also do more of those other things. We'll use our capital to broaden our business, and we will be able to attract really talented people away from the big firms who will come with adjusted expectations.

The biggest problem the people in our industry succumbed to was getting their W-2 and their IQ confused, but they're sorting that out. People will work for less; they will work harder, and they will think out of the box and be creative. There is plenty to do in this environment because you have companies that are going to fail, companies that will need restructuring, and companies that will succeed by rolling up other companies. There's going to be a lot going on. The 1970s were a difficult time but a lot happened; and you could make a lot of money in the 1970s. I think we are going to return to that type of environment.

Looking for Opportunity

Like many other people, we assess what's going on and where we should be every day. Sometimes a very obvious opportunity arises, like our decision to be in credit space; and now we're in it. Some other opportunities are a little more subtle. For instance, the big investment banks are capital constrained today because they have to deleverage. That means the amount of money that they have on their proprietary trading desks to facilitate bond transactions and option transactions are simply not there. So there are voids that we can fill. This becomes a function of finding the right people to partner with. We get general ideas about things we want to do, and then we see if we can find people who fit those ideas. If we do, we try to explore it. There's going to be a re-equalization in this country during which we are going to have to convert debt to equity and are going to have to rebuild balance sheets. This means the underwriting business will come back at some point. You have to figure out how to be in that business and how to provide advice.

Going Forward to the Past

I have friends who are CEOs at some big companies, and they are generally not interested in talking to a younger person from one of the big firms because they think there's an ulterior motive. They believe that person wants to write a ticket, get paid, and move on. They think the person doesn't really care what happens. The future of business will be based on the past. The 1960s and 1970s—the days of people like Felix Rohatyn and Pete Peterson, who gave advice that sometimes resulted in business but sometimes did not—will come back. I predict a more client-oriented business than it has been, something for which we've already seen evidence. We saw Gleacher Partners merge into this little public company called Broadpoint Securities, wherein the CEO took his advisory business and merged it to a broker-dealer. Investment management firm Citadel just hired a bunch of bankers from Merrill Lynch, and Fortress is looking for people like that as well. Many of us believe this is where it's going and are trying to get ahead. You just have to figure out where to put your first stake in the ground.

Examples of Keeping Your Mind and Brain Open to Good Ideas

You can't design time frames. You can get lucky and accomplish something very quickly, or it may take years to complete. Who knows. What I do know is you have to show up every day at work; you have to be there every day to find opportunity. You have to be constantly alert to what the possibilities are. Good ideas are all around all the time, if you're paying attention.

I can think of many examples of this; a funny one occurred in October 1995. It was 5:00 A.M., and I was up watching a CNBC interview with the CEO of a company named Magna Copper. He couldn't have been more boring. The interviewer said, "So Mr. So-and-So, yesterday you reported earnings were up 100 percent for the quarter; what can we expect looking forward?" And the fellow replies, "Well, I don't know exactly, but probably for the next eight quarters we would expect similar comparisons. We opened up this mine in Peru, and the results are better than expected; and this mine in Arizona is better than expected." He went on to discuss a few more issues. He was factual but flat. Yet I'm listening to this, and I think, "Did I really just hear what this man just said?"

So I go in the office, and I find Magna Copper. The stock is $17 a share. It's a convertible preferred, with a 4 percent dividend, trading flat—no premium for the convertible. I did a little research, and based on what this fellow said, this company is selling at two times the future cash flow. So I buy some of the preferred stock, and I'm getting paid a dividend of $4 while I own the stock. Meanwhile, I have some research done and develop an investment view. This went on for two or more months. I kept adding to it. The stock crept a little bit higher, a little bit higher, and just before Christmas, again I am in the apartment watching TV and along comes a breaking news flash from CNBC. It says Magna Copper is being acquired by Broken Hill, a big Australian mining company, for $34 a share.

This fellow being interviewed on CNBC—whose name I cannot recall—proved my point about paying attention. I made 100 percent of my money on what was a pretty meaningful position for me, and it was because I was up listening at 5:00 A.M. and paid attention to a mining executive talking about copper, which at the time was not very exciting.

There was another time when I took my eight-year-old son (now 31 and working for Ramius) to buy sneakers. We were in the shoe store, and as we were buying a pair of New Balance sneakers, my son begins telling me about how the Nike Air Jordans are *the* thing. So I ask him, "Well, why aren't you buying the Air Jordans?" He replied, "Because I have a fat foot, Dad, and they aren't comfortable on me. The New Balance is a better sneaker for me; but I'm telling you, this Nike shoe is a big deal."

So as we were leaving the store, he asks me, "How much is a share of Nike?" I happened to know the answer, because we used to be Nike's bankers (this was back in the Shearson Lehman days). I told him that it was around $12 a share. He told me he had $300 saved up from walking a dog every day for a $1 a day. He asked if he could buy 100 shares of Nike and wanted to know how much it would be. I said to him, "Well, you figure it out," and he came up with the correct response, $1,200. And then he asked if I would lend him $900—and I agreed. So I put the $900 in his account, he gave me his $300, and we bought 100 shares of Nike.

But now he has my attention. So I start asking, what's going on with this Air Jordan? Anyway, fast-forward to late December of 1991, we sold the stock at around $71 per share. Profitable information can come from the least expected places, like shoe shopping with an eight-year-old.

My son mentioned another idea—much bigger than Nike—when he was around 15 years old, when he started discussing the Human Genome Project. Although he was never very big on science, he started talking to me about the genome project and mapping genes, what that was going to mean, and about this company in Rockville, Maryland, called Human Genome Sciences. We looked it up, and it was $14 per share. We bought some stock, and I started to pay more attention to it. We added to it. That stock went to $450 before it was all over.

So I'll take information wherever I get it and run it down. Winning is all about showing up. I know a lot of people who say they don't want to go to work and claim to have nothing to do there. That's not true. There is always something to do at work—always. That is a philosophy that I follow, and that we follow. And while I think we're in for a really difficult time ahead, I'm really excited that there'll be some great opportunities that will come out of it.

11

When I started to assign my contacts to chapters in my book, a lot of them asked me not to put them in "Chapter 11," which is commonly known as a "reorganized" bankruptcy. General Motors and Chrysler are the two big examples in this financial fallout. No CEO wants his or her name associated with the words "Chapter 11." So instead, I have opted not to highlight anyone in this chapter. So let's turn the page, and go to Chapter 12.

12

Jerry York

When people hear the name Jerry York, they think of his experience in the auto industry. York once served as a chief aide to billionaire investor Kirk Kerkorian and his Tracinda Investment Company. In a January 2006 speech at the Detroit Auto Show, York recommended a "drastic" rebuild at GM that included dumping its Saab and Hummer divisions (sound familiar?). He claimed that "Saab and Hummer will not save GM."

One month later, Kerkorian helped York get elected to the board of directors of General Motors in an effort to represent Tracinda's 9.9 percent investment in the auto

(*continued*)

(continued)
company. He wanted to turn GM around and was also hoping that this move would form an alliance with Renault-Nissan. On October 6, 2006, after GM ended talks with Renault-Nissan, York resigned from the board. In his resignation letter, he said he had "grave reservations concerning the ability of the company's current business model to successfully compete in the marketplace with those of the Asian producers."

But contrary to this association, Jerry is more than autos. He is the chairman and CEO of the private investment company Harwinton Capital, which specializes in technology, biotechnology, and real estate. Jerry helped lead the turnaround at IBM when he served as the CFO for the company from 1993 to 1995. He also held other executive positions at Chrysler and currently sits on the boards of Apple, Tyco International Ltd., and Dana Holdings Corporation.

Sitting down with Jerry gave me the opportunity to see how truly thoughtful he is. One can hear him weigh the words as he speaks.

The credit crisis began unfolding in the summer of 2007, and I was greatly concerned. In fact, I decided in June and July of that year to significantly lighten up on the equities that I owned. I told my various account managers and sold 40 percent of the equities that I owned at that time. I put a substantial amount of that money into municipal securities and left some of it in cash.

Fundamentally, the money that stayed in equities was the shares of companies on whose boards I sit; I also held onto a lot of energy stocks at that point in time. So it's as though I told Mr. Money Manager to hang on to these and sell the rest.

Analyzing the Situation

I had become very concerned about the potential impact of tightened lending standards on business activity. I felt it could lead to some very significant slowdowns in the economy. Interestingly, in March 2008, I gave the keynote speech at *CFO Magazine*'s annual event, and I presented quite a negative view. One thing I cautioned to the various financial executives in attendance was the need to understand their counter party risk and any derivative instruments that they have. One of the top folks at *CFO Magazine* called me out late in the summer of 2008 and said, "My God, you really nailed this thing." I replied, "No, actually; I was too optimistic." By the time I received that call, the Bear Stearns situation was looking grim, and of course, shortly thereafter the Lehman Brothers' meltdown occurred.

Lehman Brothers' Downfall and Managing through the Turmoil

I assumed that the situation with Lehman Brothers would be similar to that with Bear Stearns; that is, I assumed the government would step in. In retrospect, it was a grave mistake for the government to let Lehman Brothers go down the tubes, because that is what really put a huge amount of fear into the economy.

At that point, I started selling more equities to lighten the load. As a result of earlier actions, I managed to get through 2008 with a negative return of 12 percent on my portfolios, which I think was pretty good in light of the market meltdown that took place from September to December. There were certainly a number of firms that had produced stellar results, but mainly by shorting the markets. You can make money no matter which way the market is going if you make the right calls. Quite frankly, I have not done too well over the years shorting the market, so I don't tend to do too much of that.

Future of Autos

This has been a draconian situation with a huge decline. It began in the U.S. market, followed shortly thereafter in the European markets, and even some of the Asian markets, most notably Japan. The drop-off in demand for autos has been nearly unprecedented. With the high fixed costs of these companies, driven by their union contracts and their heavy investment requirements to be competitive in the business, it has just been a total meat grinder for them.

The $64,000 question right now is: How much collateral damage is there going to be in the supply base? Metaldyne and Visteon Corp. both filed for bankruptcy on May 28, 2009. They unfortunately were not alone. The question that now remains is how many more auto parts makers will file?

Credit Is King

Credit is vital to any big-ticket consumer item, and my sense is that it is very slowly starting to loosen up. However, it is nowhere near as available as it used to be. There has been nothing since the Great Depression that has been anything like what's going on now.

Investing Criteria

My investing criteria depend on the particular type of security in which I'm placing funds. For example, I tend to invest heavily in municipal securities. I stay away from municipal securities issued by institutions and states that are under extreme pressure. I do not own any Michigan, New Jersey, or California municipal securities. I prefer to stick to the states that don't have serious budget problems.

As far as equities go, it's best in this type of market to stay away from anything where revenues are dependent on credit availability. Any time I buy a stock, I also look at the maturity schedule of any debt they have on their balance sheet. It's a cautionary sign if they have any material debt maturities in the next 12 to 18 months. You probably don't want to buy that type of equity.

My investing time frame is long term; I am not a trader in equities. I like to buy stocks and hold them for three to five years. I don't like to talk to my investment advisers every week, so to speak. I like to own stocks that I am very, very comfortable with on a longer-term basis.

I think it is too early to be optimistic at this point. The market from the time of Lehman Brothers' bankruptcy until probably the end of February 2009 was just an absolute meltdown. But on the other hand, I think most people, myself included, are definitely sleeping better now than we were a few months ago.

Part Two

BANKING

13

Kelly King

Since the fall of Bear Stearns and Lehman Brothers, the term *bank* has become a dirty word. The historic $700 billion "financial" industry bailout in the fall of 2008 acted as the backdrop for well-known CEOs losing their jobs, and banks failing and being seized by the Federal Deposit Insurance Corporation (FDIC) as a common Friday occurrence. Fears of "is my money safe?" were rampant after Wachovia and Washington Mutual failed. Then, in order to restore confidence, the FDIC raised the limit of deposit insurance on U.S. bank accounts from $100,000 to $250,000 per depositor.

But during this turmoil, a part of the industry was trying to thrive—regional banks. I remember driving in to work in the fall of 2008 and the winter of 2009 seeing signs such as "Still Strong, Still Lending" hanging above their doors. One

(*continued*)

(continued)

of the regional bank chief executive officers attempting to lead through this new economy is BB&T Corporation CEO Kelly King.

BB&T is no stranger to the conditions of the crisis we're facing right now. In fact, the bank successfully operated during the Great Depression. Kelly has been with the company since 1972 and began his tenure as CEO in January 2009 in the middle of the credit crisis. He had served as BB&T's chief operating officer since 2004.

I met Kelly through one of my great financial contacts, Donald Powell (who you'll be reading about a little later). Don was guest co-hosting a one-hour exclusive special on *Squawk Box*—a regional banking summit. On the panel was Kelly King. My pre-interview with him for the show was great, and I knew in my gut he would be an amazing guest. My gut is rarely wrong.

So why did I choose to include Kelly's—and BB&T's—story in my book, rather than other regional banks? It was a no-brainer; BB&T has adequate capital on its balance sheet for acquisitions, meaning it is in good health and poised to grow during this time. The bank was "asked" to accept Troubled Asset Relief Program (TARP) money along with the country's other 18 largest banks and underwent the stress test. It was one of only nine that "passed" the test and therefore was not required to raise additional capital. After the stress test results were announced, BB&T said it would raise $1.5 billion, along with a large dividend cut and existing cash, to pay off the $3.1 billion it received in TARP funding. The bank was cleared by the government to pay back its TARP money and exited the Troubled Asset Relief Program on June 17, 2009 when it paid the U.S. Treasury with interest.

Nearly two months later, Montgomery, Alabama–based Colonial Bank, one of BB&T's rivals, failed and was seized by the FDIC on August 14. BB&T then purchased Colonial's loans, deposits, and most of its assets from the government. At that time, Colonial Bank was the sixth-largest bank failure in U.S. history. This acquisition gave BB&T further access to the Florida and Alabama markets, which is part of its growth strategy. The structure of the deal also shielded BB&T from potential losses when the FDIC agreed to share losses with BB&T on $14 billion of the $22 billion in assets included in this deal.

Although initially Kelly was shocked by the events at Bear Stearns and Lehman Brothers, he is optimistic on the future of banking.

I was very surprised to hear about the Bear Stearns mess because, just a few years earlier, I had been in New York and had a nice hour-long chat with "Ace" Greenberg, the former chairman of the Executive Committee of The Bear Stearns Companies. We had a genuinely good discussion about our companies' similarities. My initial surprise was followed by shock when I realized the magnitude of the subprime mess in Bear Stearns' entire global portfolio. The reason I was surprised is because BB&T did not offer subprime mortgages; we were not participating in that profit flow. In fact, most commercial banks like us were not. The magnitude of what was going on in the securitization market, particularly around Residential Mortgage Backed Securities (RMBS)* really astonished me.

As the Bear Stearns debacle played out, it crystallized for me what a major problem we had. If a firm of the reputation, stature, and experience of Bear Stearns can be taken out of the game literally overnight, there had to be some major and unusual—not to mention dangerous—forces at play.

---

* *Author's note:* Residential Mortgage Backed Securities are securities with coming cash flow from residential debt. RMBS are a type of mortgage backed security.

The Call to Let Lehman Brothers Fail

It was a pretty risky step for the government to step in and subsidize the Bear Stearns transaction, because that meant it was clearly heading down a slippery slope in terms of expanding the "too big to fail" concept.

But when the government let Lehman Brothers go, I thought it was the right thing. Bear Stearns caught the government totally by surprise, at least in my view. Out of shock, it's reaction was, "We cannot let them fail"; and so it put a deal together overnight. When it let Lehman Brothers go, as bad as it was—and as traumatic as I thought it would be—I still believe that the government made the right move. What startled me, however, was when the government came right behind Lehman Brothers and bailed out AIG. It appeared as though the government was flip-flopping, or picking winners and losers. It became increasingly frustrating to see not only how big this problem was but how misguided our government was in trying to deal with it.

Did the government really develop a strategic plan for dealing with the problem? Did the government really even know how big a problem it was? Was it honest about how large a role politics was playing in its decision making? (From my vantage point, it certainly looked like politics was a big part of it.)

But one of the things I've learned after being in business for 37 years is to be careful about second-guessing people who have really hard decisions to make when I may not have all the facts. Even though I had real reservations about their decisions, I had respect for former Treasury Secretary Henry Paulson and Fed Chairman Ben Bernanke, and certainly appreciated the fact that this was an extremely tumultuous situation. I gave them the benefit of the doubt and assumed there must be a lot more to it than I knew.

All of this turmoil left the market feeling very uneasy. We saved Bear Stearns, let Lehman Brothers fail, and then saved AIG. So how big is this problem and exactly how are we dealing with it? The market certainly didn't understand why we saved two and let one fail. It didn't understand the pervasiveness of the problem. All of that contributed significantly to the nervousness in the market. The crescendo of panic that started setting in gave way to an enormous liquidity scare for the next year or so.

Using History as a Guide

At BB&T, we hunkered down and tried to figure out where the industry might be heading from here, including worst-case scenarios. Certainly, when IndyMac Federal Bank failed, and we watched TV coverage of lines of people wrapped around the parking lot waiting to find out where their money was, we knew a massive depreciation in the financial services industry was a possibility.

We did not have any particular concerns about our own company. We've always tried to manage very conservatively, probably because of our past. As you may know, our bank is 137 years old. During the Great Depression, BB&T in Wilson, North Carolina, was the only bank in the Carolinas that stayed open amid all the other bank failures and disasters of that period. So a big part of our heritage is literally surviving a bank panic.

In fact, at the height of the Great Depression—when people were coming in and taking out all of their money—they would go to the post office in Wilson and convert their money into postal money orders. They didn't know that the post office banked with us too! So you had people taking their money out of our bank and going to the post office to get a money order. Then at night, the post office would turn around and bring the money right back over to our bank. It kept circulating between BB&T and the post office. And we never closed our doors.

Because of that heritage, we've always believed in being really conservative and being prepared for any major crisis. And that's exactly what has occurred since the problems in our industry began to unravel in 2008. When the worst of the liquidity crisis was happening, nobody would lend money to anybody. In fact, there were organizations bringing money to us at 0 percent interest. We'd tell them we didn't need the money, and they'd reply, "That's fine; we just want to put it in your bank."

So other organizations viewed us as a safe haven throughout the ordeal, which was of course rewarding for us. However, I continued to worry about the financial system as a whole. Our financial system is based on faith, and when the American public loses faith in the financial system and the government's ability to support it, it could lead to an absolute collapse across the industry.

Being Prepared for a Crisis

You obviously have to be ready for a crisis; it's too late when events are already underway. So even though we were very strong, we continued to do all we could to prepare. For example, we built up our liquidity—not just to make sure we had enough, but also so we'd be able to access it throughout that entire period. Our executive team was meeting at least once a day, just to be sure we had our fingers on the pulse of everything occurring across the company. Obviously, it was the most challenging environment of my career, unlike anything I'd ever seen.

What Went Wrong

Three things truly "went wrong": First, we, the American public overconsumed, overspent, undersaved, underproduced, and levered ourselves to the hilt over the past 30 years. The consuming public had a role to play and therefore a lesson to learn.

Second, our government took the public policy position that everybody should own a home. And because it so aggressively pushed that policy, it did substantial damage to the investment community and the banking community, not to mention now-bankrupt Freddie

Mac and Fannie Mae. Third, the financial services industry made mistakes too. Although our own bank fortunately did not, the industry as a whole created some rather complex and sophisticated products. In doing so, it created a mechanism that allowed the country to lever itself without fully contemplating the consequences of doing so. Finally, the regulatory community did not develop the sophisticated regulatory processes that were needed.

But all of that doesn't mean that America is bad, far from it. It just means we made some big mistakes that we'll have to learn from. It means we have an opportunity now to come out of this and be a great country in the future like we've been in the past. What will make the difference going forward is leadership, specifically leadership in business and government at all levels. Ultimately, when it comes to big decisions, leadership always makes the difference.

After all, even though a lot of the discussion of late has been about capital—capital shortages and so forth—you can give bad leaders with bad strategies all the capital in the world and they'll blow it. But if you give capital to good leaders who know how to develop good strategies, they will effectively use it to provide a reasonable return to investors.

Have there been any lessons learned from this crisis at the governmental level? Maybe. At the regulatory level? I hope so. At the business community level? *Absolutely.* That's because the business community does not have the luxury of printing money and saying things without any culpability. In a free market system, when the business community makes mistakes, we pay the price.

I was talking to the CEO of a major bank that failed recently and asked him how he was doing. He said, "You know, I'm doing fine. I made a really terrible big debt acquisition in my company and I paid the price for it. But it was my mistake—it was a leadership failure—and I'm learning from that and moving on." The reality is that companies rise or fall based largely on their leadership. Bad decisions by leaders can have disastrous results. We've certainly seen that lately.

Taking TARP

In the beginning, the George W. Bush Administration decided that the financial situation was so dire that they needed to step in and take action. So they injected capital into the healthy banks to stabilize the financial system and to stimulate lending from those institutions. But the way it was presented to Congress was surreal. In essence, Congress was told that, "The Treasury is going to give money to healthy banks so that they can make more loans."

I have told people repeatedly that I have never seen one short sentence with so many inaccuracies in it. First of all, they didn't *give* any money to anybody. It was a preferred stock investment with a 5 percent amortized coupon, which was very expensive. The administration also said they were going to give it to only the healthy banks, which wasn't at all the case because they gave it to a lot of unhealthy banks as well. And then they said they were putting the money in the healthy banks so that they would make more loans. But the healthy banks were already making loans! So nothing in the aforementioned statement was accurate, and the problem it caused was this: Congress heard that these banks were getting this money so that they would make more loans. Congress interpreted this as: "Now they'll have to make the kind of loans we want them to make." The next thing you know, the public is hearing from Congress and the administration that TARP money is taxpayer money and the banks are supposed to be out there granting any and all loans.

So when every John Doe on the street didn't get the loan he wanted, regardless of whether those loans made any sense or not, he ranted and raved to Congress that banks weren't doing what they were supposed to be doing with this "free" taxpayer money. And it turned into a convoluted mess because it was so poorly presented and explained.

BB&T has said all along that we never needed nor wanted any TARP money. But it was very clear from Treasury and regulators that we were expected to take the money. The way it was presented even to us was that all the healthy banks would be getting this money. So if BB&T was the only healthy bank that didn't take any, it might appear as though we weren't a healthy bank. And since we couldn't take that risk, we took the money.

At first of course, there were no strings attached to TARP/Capital Purchase Plan (CPP) money. It was simply a preferred stock investment. But as everything unfolded over the months following, there was a buildup of enormous negative sentiment. The average person on the street began to believe that banks are bad and that TARP banks are really bad. As the story continued to unfold, the stimulus bill—with its onerous compensation limitations—came along. Then there was all the rhetoric coming out of Washington about things like employee recognition events and other normal business activities, just more unexpected entanglements that came with TARP. My biggest concern was that government money in banks could politicize the lending process. That's destructive for any company, and for the economy as a whole.

Another unfortunate part of this story is that the government makes you take this money, and then it makes you wait for approval to pay the money back. We received approval in early June 2009 to pay back the TARP money, certainly a milestone in all of this from our perspective. In addition to paying the principal, we had to negotiate with the government to retire the warrants. So when it was all said and done, we paid back more than the initial $3.1 billion investment plus a final dividend payment of approximately $13.9 million. Our total dividend payments under TARP were around $92.7 million. BB&T also took a charge of about $48 million in the second quarter of 2009 for the difference between the amortized cost of the preferred stock and the repurchase price.

Public Backlash

The public backlash lingered for quite some time. One June weekend I was talking to someone who asked me what I did for a living. When I told him I was a banker, he asked me snidely, "Did you guys take any of that TARP money?" Again, the public perception is that TARP banks are the worst of the breed. And I don't blame the public for that sentiment, because I understand how they came to that conclusion. They heard their presidents, other members of the Bush and Obama administrations, and Congress say over and over that banks were the problem and the creators of this mess. The American public has also heard that until we fix the bad banks, we cannot get the economy going. Too many people unfortunately believe anything that comes out of Washington. So although I can understand the perspective of the American public, that misperception puts us in a terrible position.

Keeping the Lines of Communication Open

For three days every June, I meet with thousands of our employees. Our management team visits and talks to our officers throughout our 11-state (13 with the Colonial acquisition) footprint. Much of our discussion in 2009 was about countering all the wrong information they had heard with the truth about what was really going on.

I want them to know that they're not bad people. I want them to know that, despite what they may read in the newspapers or hear on the radio or see on TV. The vast majority of all the banks in this country are still doing the really good wholesome work we've always done. We're out there granting loans to people so that they can achieve their dreams, goals, and hopes in life. We're protecting their deposits and providing them with financial products and services, such as insurance and small business loans. So we do really good work.

In addition to that, our employees spend thousands of hours working in the community with their local United Way and countless other charitable organizations. In fact, on September 30, 2009, our employees wrapped up an inspiring two-month community service initiative called the BB&T Lighthouse Project, the largest philanthropic effort in our 137-year history. Working in teams, employees across our corporation selected over 1,000 organizations in their local markets and helped over one million people. Our employees volunteered more than 40,000 hours painting, building, and repairing homes; participating in homeless prevention programs; conducting school supply drives and food drives; and more. We set aside $3 million and gave employees time off to carry out their projects.

These employees should never feel bad about themselves or our industry. I tell them they should be very proud of themselves, the company they work for, and their industry. It helps to hear a positive reinforcement of the truth. My biggest concern, though, is this: How do we get the American public to understand the truth?

Thriving Game Plan

To come up with a BB&T game plan, we sat down and decided that we have to be crystal clear about what our immediate priorities are. Number one, we are in a short-term, focused strategic mind-set. Number two, liquidity is absolutely our biggest priority. Number three, capital is the next priority. Number four is profitability.

That order is somewhat unusual, because in the long term, profitability is really important. But I made it very clear to our team that in the short term, liquidity rises to the top of the list. Right behind that is strength of capital. If we had to deplete profitability in order to shore up liquidity and capital that would absolutely be the right thing to do to survive.

Strategically, we had to make sure that our people were fully aware of what was going on as best we knew it. We increased our communication with our employees so that they wouldn't panic over what they were hearing on the street. Everybody watches and reads the news, and hears what's going on. We had 1,500-plus financial centers at the time and 30,000 employees. I wanted to be sure that those employees did not assume the worst based on what they were hearing.

So we increased our communication with our entire employee base. We told them exactly what we knew and reminded them again and again of how strong we were. We told them we did not have any liquidity concerns or capital concerns, and that regardless of how bleak the news may look, we were totally confident that we would get through everything fine. We also stressed to them that the country would get through it fine and that, in the end, we would have all gone through a tough learning experience we would ultimately grow from.

We were very focused on communication because we realized that employees want to hear from top management as much as possible, but never more so than when times are tough. In addition to having myself and our top leaders address our employees, we also felt it was important to hear directly from them. So we invited them to send in any questions or concerns, and we answered as many as we could on our intranet and internal video.

Seizing the Opportunities

Being right in the backyard of (the former) Wachovia, we immediately started seeing business opportunities. Wachovia started having problems pretty early on as all of this unfolded. The history between Wachovia and BB&T dates back 100 years. Both companies competed against each other, stemming from the fact that legacy Wachovia was headquartered in Winston-Salem, where BB&T is headquartered now.

Legacy Wachovia and BB&T have always been viewed as very conservative and solid commercial banks. When legacy Wachovia sold itself to First Union in 2001 (First Union took the Wachovia name), the merger created a lot of turmoil, primarily because First Union and legacy Wachovia were almost 180 degrees apart in terms of culture and strategy. When the merger went through, everybody in business viewed it as a potential opportunity—not that anybody at that time expected the combined organization to fail, but it was clear it was going to be a tough merger to put together.

Then in mid-2008, as the new Wachovia appeared to be on the verge of failing, we began to see a huge rush of legacy Wachovia clients coming to BB&T. They knew how similar our two organizations were. They had stayed with the new Wachovia after the merger because they wanted to give the combined organization a chance. But then during the merger process, many of the legacy Wachovia employees were let go. So when the financial problems started occurring, the employees—and the relationships—simply weren't there. On top of that, there were questions about the new company's financial stability. With all of that as the backdrop, we soon began to see a lot of business flow over to us from Wachovia.

We have seen the same kind of thing play out with other institutions, such as Bank of America, although Wachovia certainly was the most pronounced example. The general turmoil in the market created additional opportunities for us. We reminded our employees that this is a difficult time in the industry, and we didn't want to be scavengers. We would never tout the difficulties that other companies were having as a means to win new business. That's never been a part of our values and culture.

On the other hand, we always owe it to our shareholders to grow our business. When your competitors are weak, you certainly try to take business away from them if you can. So we stepped up our effort to call on the clients of the companies that were having trouble. We reinforced our position in the marketplace, stressing that we were the oldest bank in the Carolinas, very strong, very sound, with a long track record of stability.

After all, we have been around for 137 years, and that resonated very well in the marketplace. Somewhere along the way, we launched an advertising campaign with a new tagline that summed it up: "BB&T, Best Bank in Town since 1872." We thought that this statement professionally emphasized our stability and our strength relative to others who couldn't honestly make that same claim.

The ad campaign worked great. We know that it led to an accelerated growth rate, and we have countless anecdotes of larger companies and individuals moving their accounts over to us. We believe that thousands of others we didn't previously know moved their business to us because of how we were describing ourselves in the marketplace. The strength and stability message was certainly the right one for the time, but I believe it actually just reinforced what the market already knew.

Growing in the New Economy

For the past 25 to 30 years, we went through a prolonged period when many traditional commercial loans left the balance sheet and went out into the capital markets through the securitization process. This is known as *disintermediation.* We are now beginning a period of what I call *reintermediation,* where a lot of that business that went into the capital markets will be returning to commercial bank balance sheets. This will probably last for a decade or so and will present a real opportunity for really strong balance sheet growth for commercial banks like BB&T. So despite the recession, there's no denying that there are numerous growth opportunities out there right now. Coming out of the recession and heading into a growth period will accentuate those opportunities.

Thriving in the new economy to me is extraordinarily exciting. I take every opportunity to remind our employees that I have never been as excited about the future of our industry and the future of BB&T as I am today. The reason I'm so energized is because we're going through this process of what I call "a return to fundamental banking."

Over the past 25 years, the disintermediation process dramatically changed the nature of banking. When I first started making loans 35 years ago, the commercial banking system (including thrifts) made about 80 percent of all the loans that were granted. Over time, it drifted down to about 30 percent. Where did the rest of the loans go? Out through the securitization process into the capital markets, where there were major problems. The investors in these capital markets products (securities) perceived, understandably, that they were buying AAA bonds; after all, that's the way they were rated. As a result, they had very little capital in their reserves to cover any deterioration in the asset quality. Of course, as we now know, they were not truly AAA bonds. They were bad loans.

So the downward pricing pressure on lending in the banking industry for the past 30 years has been enormous. The same loan that I made 35 years ago in Charlotte, North Carolina—until recently—went down in price by 300 basis points, or 3 percent. That is a dramatic change. So the banking industry was defeated in two ways. We lost in volume, and the spreads were beaten down because of the securitization process.

However, we're now preparing to undergo this reintermediation process, a return to fundamental banking. We'll see more volume coming back, at better prices, and actually with better structured terms. So our future in lending looks dramatically better. And although not as dramatic, our future also looks significantly brighter on the liability side. More people are taking their money out of the stock market and putting it back in their banks to invest in CDs. I have heard many people over these years, particularly senior citizens, say, "I would never take money out of the bank and put it in the stock market." But they were actually putting their money in mutual funds; they simply never understood that meant they *were* investing in the stock market. Sadly, they lost an enormous amount of their principal, and we're seeing them by the thousands come back out of the stock market. They're putting their money back into CDs, where they can get a lower, but fair rate and feel safe and secure in their deposits. In the future, this reintermediation will help us on the loan and the deposit side.

Another piece of exciting news from our company's point of view is that this huge economic crisis is creating a shakeout and separation between weaker and stronger banks. Many of the weaker banks have closed, and will continue to fail, until this ongoing consolidation process is completed. So there will be far fewer regional players in the marketplace, therefore making the competition better and healthier. The result is more volume, better spreads, and less irrational competition, something that seems quite promising to me.

Looking toward the future, the only thing that tempers my optimism slightly is my grave concern about the trend coming out of Washington. Although I think our economy is poised to emerge from this recession and experience a number of years of solid and steady economic growth, that outlook can and will be dramatically changed if we stray away from the fundamentals of capitalism. The government is now running parts of industry and is getting more and more involved. I am afraid market forces will not be allowed to work independently. That is very, very scary to me.

However, I'm an optimist, and I believe that Americans will make the right choices in selecting their leaders to counter these trends. Hopefully, we'll become more balanced in terms of putting a focus back on the principles that have made this country so great, specifically freedom, capitalism, and free enterprise.

Thriving Criteria

We consider several things here, the first of which are our strategic objectives in terms of how we want our balance sheet to look. Once we decide on the asset structure we want going forward, we then analyze specific asset decisions. We do a very sophisticated internal return cash-flow analysis to decide on the types of investments we want to make. Similar to the process we use with acquisitions, it is a very complicated cash-flow analysis. It's less complicated with a new building or something similar, but still pretty sophisticated.

If it's a loan, you're looking at the internal rate of return on that loan, based on the capital allocated. Bottom line, our approach is to look at the risk-adjusted return on capital.

14

Donald Powell

We all know the wheels of credit freezing up created the mess we're in now. However, there is lending going on in the banking industry. The person whom I contact the most to gain perspective and knowledge in financials is former Federal Deposit Insurance Corporation (FDIC) Chairman Donald Powell. Don was sworn in as the eighteenth FDIC chair and served from 2001 to 2005. Don took the helm at the FDIC just weeks before the 9/11 terrorist attacks and one month after one of the nation's most costly

(*continued*)

(*continued*)
bank failures of the past decade. The staff back then had been cut in half because of consolidation of the banking industry, but Don was up to the challenge.

Don Powell is no stranger to adversity. His bank, the First National Bank of Amarillo, almost failed in the late 1980s. But due to the strategies he will outline in this chapter, he was able to get his company back on track. In June 2009, Don was elected to the board of Bank of America. Federal regulators urged Bank of America to recruit new board members who had both "risk management and financial services expertise." Don was one of four new directors elected five weeks after shareholders ousted CEO Ken Lewis as chairman. Don has always been vocal about his concerns about many issues, including the makeup and regulatory measurements of capital, the lack of accountability of the credit agencies, and the lack of competitors in the space. Don has maintained his long-held opinion that "too-big-to-fail" is not good public policy. "All institutions should be held to the same standards." However, Don also recognizes the importance of the systemic risk. A credit card bank failed when he was FDIC chair, and he had to devise a plan for how to close the book on the cardholders.

Don says a well thought out game plan is necessary to limit downside. . . .

The events of 9/11 occurred within weeks of my arrival at the FDIC, and as a result, the banking industry played a very important role in protecting national security. The crisis was not a normal banking crisis of safety and soundness, but rather a concern about terrorists using the banking system to finance their activities. There was real concern that they might attempt to dismantle the financial structure of America. So we at the FDIC—together with other banking regulators and the Treasury—were dealing with the issue of how to protect the nation's banking system against threats to national security. Today's crisis is more about economic and financial fundamentals, not a national security concern. It's a different economic crisis than the one following 9/11, because this one extended beyond U.S. markets. The global economy was in a severe recession.

From a banking perspective, there were many concerns, including liquidity in a depression-era type of run on banks. We saw evidence of that at IndyMac Federal Bank and at other banks as well. It was interesting in that people did not want cashier's checks; they wanted cash. There were widespread concerns about money, and people wanted cash in hand.

Uncle Sam to the Rescue

The markets wanted the government to intercede and to support liquidity and the safety of deposits in financial institutions. The Federal Reserve did many positive things, and the FDIC's insurance of all transaction accounts was extremely positive. People didn't have to worry about going to the bank and getting their money. And although some did, this measure still brought a lot of stability to the marketplace.

Thriving in the New Economy

Capital, capital, and capital! A liquidity crisis is a crisis only if you have asset quality problems; therefore banks that did not have asset quality problems did not have liquidity problems. Banks that have an abundance of capital can always weather a liquidity crisis or an asset quality crisis. This is not a fun time to be in the banking business, especially the past couple of years. The fall of 2008 was hopefully the low point, and there was a lot of panic in the marketplace during that time.

Planning Ahead

The most important thing is to have a plan. Everybody in the organization, including all stockholders, must understand what you're doing too. Then you have to execute, and you have to be disciplined about it. You cannot panic. You cannot give up. You cannot go back and second-guess; you must go forward. You have to make sure people believe in your plan, not only the shareholders or those who supply additional capital, but your employee base and, of course, your customers. If the team members are not believers, and doubt the plan's effectiveness in any way, you will fail.

Qualities of a Leader

Leadership is vital; it provides hope and stability. We usually know it when we see it. Leaders don't panic. Leaders have ice in their veins. Leaders are disciplined and have a plan—and they execute. If the facts change, they change their course. Leaders set the tone, and more importantly, they lead through example . . . they walk the talk!

Leaders must be able to stand the heat. They sometimes have to look people in the eye and say, we thought about doing that and decided not to participate, because we think a product/action has abnormal risk and would not be long-term beneficial to our shareholders. That is hard to do, especially when there is much pressure to perform with peers, but leaders don't follow the crowd; and sometimes these decisions can have consequences.

Future of Banking

In the future, commercial banking will return to a more meat and potatoes or more basic method of operating, and it won't participate in exotic products that they really don't understand or appreciate. They will revert to accepting deposits and making loans. Of course, there will always be services such as insurance, trust, and other noninterest products that they'll continue to offer to customers; and although the large institutions will always be involved in some measure of investment banking, they too will be more cautious. I predict that we are going to put a premium on capital, and we are not going to worry about increasing our earnings per share every quarter. We are going to make more decisions based on long-term rather than short-term focus. We are going to have long-term rewards, something that shareholders will recognize, appreciate, and understand. And management will start changing the way they manage.

The Untold Story

There may be an untold story here, which is that we need to remind ourselves that the banking business is not going to go away. It is critical to the free enterprise system. It is one of the fundamental pillars of American life. We must have a banking system. We need to do some things differently, of course, but those who would say banks are going to go away are simply wrong. They're going to be around, and they're going to be around forever.

Game On

Here's the game plan: There are always going to be business cycles. People will say "This time is different." "The same thing is not going to happen to us." "Our conditions are different." "We have controls in place." Well, that's not true. There are always going to be ups and downs. Those who prepare for, recognize, and understand that fact will survive. A strong balance sheet—that is, one that is not leveraged and the capital section is "paid in capital" and "retained earnings"—is critical. You also can't get caught up in the wind of, "Well, everybody's doing it" or "We have to be in the game when the game is being played." That should not be the reasoning. Judgment, intellect, and common sense will play a vital role going forward. We tend to forget what we've learned from the past; and although this crisis will pass, we cannot forget the painful lessons it taught.

I used to give speeches when I was at the FDIC about how now is the time to make tough decisions, because you'll be forced to make them in bad times and that's not the time to do it. I mean everybody reduces the workforce during a downturn; everybody restricts their capital expenditures. Everybody cuts advertising. But it's best to do that when you are doing well. There are always going to be down times. Yet we never seem to learn that lesson. There is always going to be a downtime. It is not up forever, and it is not down forever.

As I stated before—and despite what some people claim—banks are not going away. Some will blame big banks, and some will blame small banks; some will blame regulators, and some will blame the Federal Reserve. But the truth is that we control our own destiny. The fact is that you need to be prepared for tomorrow. It's going to be worse, and you're the only one who can do anything about it.

Banks, including the one I worked at in the 1980s, have undoubtedly done some dumb things. At the time, we didn't think our actions were dumb, but even at the time we made certain decisions, we knew we were taking unusual risk. But we thought, "Gosh, this economy is so good, we can't make a mistake." I remember being concerned during the oil crisis of the 1980s and telling my wife that I wasn't sure we would always be able to buy fuel for our automobile. I remember waiting in line to fill my car and recalling the fact that oil is a depleting asset. No alternative product was in sight, and demand was strong; and yet oil plummeted to less than $15.00 a barrel. Don't ever say certain things can't happen, because anything can happen. And you need to keep that in mind while you're planning for the future.

This is a defining moment; we will never be the same after this. Psychologists often say that you have five or six defining moments in your life. This is a defining moment in the economic life of America. We cannot let this downturn paralyze us or question our trust in the free enterprise system. We have to live; but we must do so with a better set of standards. Again, the problem is judgment; we must learn from our irresponsible behavior. You are always going to have downturns in a free enterprise system, but they do not last forever. It's like that old saying: You can't have a rainbow until it rains.

15

Cam Fine

Cam Fine is president and CEO of the Independent Community Bankers of America (ICBA), which is the national trade association that represents community banks. But he is not an association CEO who has never had skin in the game. Prior to joining the ICBA, Cam was president and CEO of Midwest Independent Bank in Jefferson City, Missouri, which he also helped found in 1985. He was also a budget analyst for the state of Missouri, and in 1981, he was appointed the director of the state Division of Taxation and Collection by former governor and current U.S. Senator Christopher "Kit" Bond. In October 2000, Cam was appointed to the Federal Advisory Council of the Board of Governors of the Federal Reserve System, representing the 10th Federal Reserve District (Kansas City).

(*continued*)

(*continued*)
Cam's knowledge and experience took him to the White House in the spring of 2009 as one of the CEOs who met with President Obama during the famous banker's meeting. Cam's outlook on the banking sector, specifically the regional banks, is insightful and offers investors a ground floor view of what's going on.

The extraordinary events that occurred in the fall of 2008 were presaged with a series of shocks to the nation's financial system that did not bode well for the more than 8,000 smaller and regional banks that constitute the community banking industry. Although the nation's financial system had been experiencing strain since the fall of 2007, the financial crisis broke out into full public view with the Federal Reserve's bailout of Bear Stearns in March 2008. The ICBA immediately condemned the Bear Stearns bailout as dangerous overreach by the Federal Reserve that potentially put thousands of community banks on the hook for the financial sins of Wall Street.

At the time, editorial writers and news show commentators generally praised the Federal Reserve, believing that the rescue of Bear Stearns would have a cathartic and stabilizing effect on Wall Street. But the pundits were wrong—and the crisis intensified into the spring and early summer of 2008. As the first quarter bank call reports and earnings announcements rolled out in late April and May, it became apparent that the financial waters were roiled. Banking institutions began to fail on a regular basis, and the crisis reached a boiling point when IndyMac failed in July 2008. It was the largest bank failure in U.S. history to that point. The public was now not only fully aware of the financial turmoil on Wall Street but also alarmed. So, too, was the ICBA and the community banking industry.

Fall 2008—A September to Remember

Black Sunday—September 7, 2008

In the weeks preceding the September 7, 2008, government seizure of Fannie Mae and Freddie Mac, warning signs were abundant that something dramatic was afoot for the two housing government-sponsored enterprises (GSEs). Rumors swirled in Washington about government takeover of the housing GSEs. Beginning about a month prior to the September weekend seizure of Fannie Mae and Freddie Mac, Federal Housing Finance Agency (FHFA) Director Lockhart and his new agency were unusually quiet. Statements from the FHFA and the Treasury were suddenly vague and less reassuring as to the health of the two housing giants. This was in sharp contrast to statements made by both Lockhart and Secretary Paulson in the spring and early summer of 2008 that both Fannie Mae and Freddie Mac were "adequately capitalized" and that any notion of a government takeover was "absurd."

Although I knew that a government seizure of the GSEs was a possibility since the July 2008 passage of HR 3221 (The Housing and Economic Recovery Act of 2008), I was surprised by the government repudiation of the GSE preferred stockholders. We were caught off guard because the Federal Reserve/Treasury had protected the preferred stockholders in the Bear Stearns bailout in March 2008; therefore, the same was expected from the Treasury after the government seizures of the housing GSEs.

The key difference between the two events (the bailout of Bear Stearns and the seizures of Fannie Mae and Freddie Mac), of course, was who held the preferred shares of the two companies. In the case of Bear Stearns, the preferred stock was held mainly by Wall Street firms, not the least of which was Goldman Sachs (Secretary Paulson's former firm) and JPMorgan Chase. In the case of the housing GSEs, the preferred shares were more broadly held, and mainly by community and regional banking institutions (the "too small to save"). The dismissive and unconcerned attitude shown by Treasury officials in their initial public statements as to the damage that might be caused by the repudiation of the preferred shareholders (mostly community banks, which held more than $25 billion in GSE preferred shares) shocked and outraged the community banking industry, to say the least. The Treasury's first public comment on the matter that "only a few smaller institutions will be affected" telegraphed a total lack of institutional knowledge within the Treasury of the community banking sector, its culture, and its ownership structure. To add insult to injury, the Treasury's actions on that black Sunday, September 7, 2008, also repudiated earlier assurances from Lockhart and several Treasury officials—including Secretary Paulson—that the GSEs were structurally sound and adequately capitalized. In fact, as late as April 2008, Lockhart was quoted as saying that a government takeover of the GSEs was "out of the question."*

Feelings of outrage and betrayal coursed through the community banking industry that September Sunday afternoon. As President and CEO of the ICBA, I immediately issued a statement on Monday morning, September 8, 2008, about the consequences to the community banking industry, Main Street America, and consumers of the government's seizure of the housing GSEs.

"Let Them Eat Cake"

Those famous words—attributed to Queen Marie Antoinette of France when told that her people were suffering and starving—perfectly sum up the seeming attitude of the top financial policy makers of the U.S. government when they learned that scores of community banks could suffer from the abrupt nationalization of

---

* *Author's note:* Lockhart's statement was made just after Fannie Mae and Freddie Mac agreed to raise equity. Lockhart has told me whatever he said was based on the assumption that they were going to be successful. Freddie never did raise the equity.

the housing GSEs. When asked about the impact on the nation's banking system, several top policy makers stated that the impact would be immaterial to the banking system—*only a few smaller banks would be hurt.* In effect, "Let them eat cake."

On Sunday, September 7, 2008—a day that will live in financial infamy—the U.S. Treasury, the Federal Reserve Board, and the newly minted Federal Housing Finance Agency (FHFA or as I call them, the Triumvirate) nationalized two of the largest financial firms in the United States. In a move that would have made Hugo Chavez proud, the top financial policy makers of the United States engineered a weekend coup and wiped out thousands of individual and institutional investors with the stroke of a pen. What's more, the takeover came despite the fact that both Fannie Mae and Freddie Mac were still adequately capitalized under statute. Perhaps these breathtaking actions were necessary, perhaps not; only time will tell. However, what is truly outrageous to the ICBA and thousands of community bankers is the cavalier attitude that top U.S. financial policy makers exhibited toward the community banking industry.

Would the Treasury, Federal Reserve, and FHFA have been as cavalier had Citigroup or JPMorgan Chase held $400 billion of GSE preferred stock? I think we all know the answer to that. The answer has been confirmed time and again during this current financial crisis. If you are a mega Wall Street firm—or if you are too "interconnected" to Wall Street or world markets—your counterparties have nothing to fear. Even your firm will be given considerable forbearance. But if you are a community bank going about your business serving your community, you are simply too small to be of concern. And if your balance sheet becomes impaired by actions of our government and through no fault of your own, well, be afraid . . . be very afraid. You are too small to worry about, my friend.

Although there is no doubt that every banker is responsible and accountable for what is on the bank's balance sheet, there is no doubt that in recent years, bankers were encouraged to diversify their assets. In many cases, regulatory examiners and outside accounting firms condoned—and in some cases, even encouraged—the purchase of GSE preferred stock as a good asset for diversification. In fact, the stock was designed by the agencies for institutional investors and even had built-in tax advantages to induce purchases—all blessed by the government regulators. So, the actions taken that weekend and the subsequent statements by our government's top financial policy makers that "only a few smaller institutions will be affected" are particularly egregious and outrageous to the scores of institutions that are affected.

Community banks are the engines that, in many regions of this nation, keep local markets going day to day. To simply write them off as inconsequential is outrageous to the ICBA and community bankers everywhere. Wall Street cheered the action because Wall Street gets what it has wanted for years: the bludgeoning to death of the GSEs, which Wall Street moneymakers have always resented. Now they have a clear field in the mortgage markets to do their will—and community bankers and consumers beware. There is now no impartial counterweight to keep the big guys honest.

To paraphrase the words of an old country song: "Wall Street got the gold; Main Street got the shaft." Every community banker in this nation, whether a member of the ICBA or not, should be extremely upset about how easily our policy makers dismiss billions of dollars of GSE equity held in community banks as "only affecting a few smaller institutions." What precedent does this set for future hits that community banks may take as the result of our government's actions?

We at the ICBA are thinking of another famous quote: "I'm as mad as hell, and I'm not going to take it anymore." Our focus is community banks and *only* community banks; and we are going to do everything in our power to protect and advance the community banking point of view on this issue and any issue of vital concern to the franchise health of all community banks. I hope all community banks—members and nonmembers alike—will join us in fighting for your franchise rights.

The response from thousands of community banks was immediate and intense. In short, they were outraged. A feeling of government betrayal followed close behind the outrage. E-mails, calls, and letters to the ICBA, the banking agencies, the Treasury, and Capitol Hill poured in by the thousands and did not let up for weeks. The mood within the community banking sector quickly turned to one of distrust of government agencies—especially the Treasury. And that sentiment has not abated to any significant degree to this day.

ICBA Grassroots Effort

The ICBA reaction to the events of September 2008 was immediate and overwhelming. On Monday morning, September 8, ICBA initiated a multifront campaign to forcefully bring community banking industry issues and concerns to the attention of key policy makers throughout Washington and to fully engage the community banking sector in the looming battles ahead. The ICBA and our affiliated state banking associations have member banks in all 435 congressional districts. The ICBA would make sure that the community banking industry and Main Street America would not be ignored in this financial crisis and that our voices would be heard by every single member of Congress and key policy makers in the bank regulatory agencies and the administration. (See Figure 15.1.)

It was clear to me and to the ICBA leadership that the Treasury's apathetic—and at times harmful—actions toward community banks were driven by a complete lack of knowledge and empathy for the community banking sector, its culture, and ownership structure. As a result, the ICBA launched an aggressive grassroots campaign to reach more than 8,000 community banks nationwide. I recorded YouTube messages to our members for immediate

Figure 15.1 ICBA Campaign

impact and recorded DVD messages for distribution to our members to use at local community group meetings—and for further distribution to influential persons and groups in their local markets.

All 44 ICBA-affiliated state banking associations were contacted and asked to coordinate their efforts with and through the ICBA. Ongoing communication with key members of Congress was significantly ramped up after the August 2008 congressional break; and after September 7, 2008, the ICBA appealed to our grassroots membership base to intensify their direct contacts with their members of Congress. These intensified contacts continued throughout the fall and to this day.

Last fall, the ICBA and our member banks touched many members of Congress in numerous ways—e-mail, direct letter mail, phone calls, and personal visits. A vigorous public media campaign, including print and media advertising, was initiated. Our communications department worked to set up interviews for me and key leadership community bankers on cable and broadcast news shows, as well as with print journalists. Our job was to heighten industry, government, and public awareness of the community banking sector, its culture, and its issues. The ICBA's job was (and is) to get the message out in a clear and forceful manner. In other words, we needed to "get in people's faces" with the community banking point of view. I saw this as my unique responsibility and challenge—and I still do.

Main Street's Economic Purpose

At the beginning of this crisis in the fall of 2007 and continuing into the fall of 2008, key policy makers at the Treasury, in the administration, and in some of the bank regulatory agencies ignored the community banking industry and Main Street America. The numerous actions taken by the Treasury and the administration in the fall of 2008 were totally centered on and for the benefit of Wall Street, regardless of the negative consequences that may befall the community banking sector or more broadly, Main Street America.

The Paulson Treasury ignored the community banking industry in the initial stages of the financial crisis. There was no institutional understanding or comprehension of the structure, culture, or ownership of community banks. In fact, it went further; there was no real appreciation for Main Street America and the banks that serve small, privately owned businesses. Everything was Wall Street–centric—from the Fed's initial response to Bear Stearns, to the Treasury's handling of the growing crisis during the summer, to the September seizure of the GSEs, to the first drafts of what would become the Troubled Asset Relief Program (TARP) bill. Nothing in any of the Treasury's actions from the fall of 2007 to the introduction of the TARP bill in mid-September of 2008 showed any recognition or understanding of the community banking sector and small business America. In short, if you were not publicly traded and a Wall Street mega firm, you were invisible to the Paulson Treasury.

My job and the ICBA's job is to transform the views and attitudes of policy makers, both on the Hill and in the administration. A changed outlook toward the community banking sector had to come quickly, or community banks would be roadkill on the financial recovery highway. My overall strategy was to convince policy makers that the community banking sector was vital to the core economy of the nation and that ignoring or harming the community banking sector also harmed small businesses and millions of consumers in thousands of smaller cities, towns, and rural areas of America. In short, policy makers needed to view the community banking sector as being vital to the nation's economic health and to the government's financial recovery efforts. To accomplish this, the ICBA needed to "bark the loudest" and become very public. I needed to drive home the point that Wall Street is not the only street in America that counts.

The ICBA Strategy

To carry out our strategy of being a relevant and active player in shaping events, the ICBA and community banks had to first be seen as the "good guys," or the "white hats." So we developed the "common sense lender" and the "safe and stable" campaigns in the spring of 2008. Coupled with our print advertisements that touted "down home values" and "relationship" banking, the ICBA promoted the picture of "heartland America," where common sense values and respect for each individual still held sway.

At the core of our current strategies for expanding the community banking sector in the new economy of the future is the notion that consumer choice and financial diversity build economic strength rather than dissipating it. That overwhelming financial concentration into the hands of a few—a financial oligarchy if you will—limits consumer choice. In addition, unwarranted government intervention, whether through direct ownership interest or through staggering regulations, weakens rather than strengthens our overall economy. As past crises and the current crisis have so bitterly demonstrated, the concentration of financial resources into the hands of a few has proved ruinous to our nation's financial health. The ICBA has pressed this point with policy makers, members of Congress, and the general public.

Through an intense public media campaign to build awareness of Main Street America, we have made Main Street America a brand—a brand that harkens back to old-fashioned common sense and values such as integrity, honesty, and caring for one's neighbors. We have used an approach of multiple communications. We have employed a strategy of "being bigger than we are"—by projecting strength and stability. In recent years, policy makers at the top positions of government have increasingly come straight from Wall Street or the mega firms. There is little or no understanding of the community banking culture, ownership structure, or "small business" nature of Main Street America. Today's policy makers are all about public companies, global finance, and "the street."

My job is to get policy makers, members of Congress, and other important constituencies to "think small," to see the "small picture" if you will. They must understand that Wall Street is not the only street that counts in America, that without the economic engines of community banks working on Main Street America, our nation's small businesses—our main creators of new jobs—will falter and fail. Community banks are "systemically important" to the smaller towns, cities, and rural areas that they serve. Ignoring the community banking sector puts our entire nation at risk.

The ICBA has been successful in our efforts to create a positive image of community banks and banking. We have succeeded in bringing these issues to the forefront in the policy debates in Washington. We have made a positive difference for the community banking industry that will have lasting effects for generations to come.

Using Proven Principles of Banking as Core Strategies Works

Why have community and smaller regional banks generally weathered the financial storm for nearly two years while mega banks have floundered? Why have most community banks seen significant deposit and loan growth? Why have earnings and return on equity been stable to growing in the majority of community banks? The answer is found in fundamental banking principles that are as old as banking itself.

Three banks illustrate this point. Although in very different markets, in reviewing the balance sheets and performance characteristics of MidSouth Bank, NA of Lafayette, Louisiana; UMB of Kansas City, Missouri; and Frost Bank of San Antonio, Texas, each of the banks share certain core banking practices that are central to running successful banking operations.

In all organizations, success begins with the leadership at the top; and MidSouth Bank, UMB, and Frost Bank each have strong, colorful, and dynamic chairmen. Each of these chairmen have impressed their values and visions on their organizations and created organizational cultures that strictly adhere to a set of very basic core values that are observed from the chairman's office to the teller window. Strong *leadership* at the top is the very first element that must be present for any business strategy to be successful.

The key strategies employed by community banks that have been a formula for success for generations (through good times and bad) and that have proved so effective during the current crisis are discussed in the following sections.

Know Your Markets and Your Products—Don't Overreach

One of the fundamental mistakes of the mega Wall Street firms is that they overreached and entered markets and initiated products of which they had little or no knowledge. The chairmen of the three banks mentioned earlier—Richard Evans of Frost Bank, Mariner Kemper of UMB Bank, and Rusty Cloutier of MidSouth Bank—all stuck to their markets and proven products. They were not tempted by quick gains to enter markets or initiate products of which they had no real knowledge.

Maintain a Strong Capital Base

Core to the community bank culture is the maintenance of a strong leverage capital base. Capital as strategy is almost a novelty to the mega Wall Street firms, but it has been employed very effectively by most community banks, including those highlighted here. Each of the community banks mentioned herein had equity capital that far exceeded regulatory minimums. As example, on March 31, 2009, Frost Bank held 12.79 percent equity capital—more than twice the regulatory requirement. The other two banks have similar profiles. Community bankers know that in a storm the safest of all harbors is capital.

Know Your Capacity for Risk and Control It Tightly

A key to succeeding in banking—whether a mega bank or a community bank—is to know your institution's capacity for risk.

In its appetite for ever-greater returns and profit, Wall Street firms seemly forgot that lesson. Certainly, UMB Bank of Kansas City never did and has pursued a conservative risk strategy that has actually seen its stock rise over the past year. Most community banks follow the UMB strategy of minimizing their risks through tight internal controls and a risk-adverse cultural bias.

Never Chase Profits

As the current crisis has so clearly illuminated, chasing profits is a fool's game. MidSouth Bank has prospered during the current financial turmoil because it pursued a reasonable profit plan and never chased profits to pump up its stock price or inflate its ratios like so many Wall Street firms did over the past decade. As a sector, community banks have long adopted a strategy of steady earnings growth built on a solid business foundation.

Don't Be on the Bleeding Edge—Never Chase Rainbows

The culture of community banking is conservative. In the eyes of most community bankers, only the foolish chase after "cutting-edge products or markets." As a strategy, community bankers like to be early adapters of new innovations, but they don't like to be on the "bleeding edge." The fundamental approach followed by the banks highlighted here has been to be a second-generation adapter, not a first-wave adapter. First-wave adapters tend to crash upon the rocks of innovation. That is not a strategy employed by community banks. Community banks do not chase rainbows.

Have a Strong-Willed Board Whose Members Understand Your Culture and Are Not Afraid to Speak Their Minds

A feature that is underappreciated by many financial services observers is that the typical community bank board is made up of strong-minded business individuals who are not afraid to speak their minds. If the boards of any of the banks highlighted here believe that their managements are pursuing flawed strategies, they are not hesitant to speak out and take action, if necessary. The key reason for this is because each board member has a personal investment and stake at risk in the institution. In most cases, community bank board members are key owners of the institution, with much of their personal net worth at stake. When you have "skin in the game," you tend to be much more alert and sensitive to what is happening in your organization.

Never Overreach or Over-Leverage Your Organization

All three banking firms mentioned here never overreach or over-leverage their firms. They know that to over-leverage a banking firm as a strategy has only one outcome in the long run: ruin! If one looks behind each financial institution's failure, you will likely find a firm that grew very rapidly and over-leveraged itself to the point of falling over. As a sector, community bankers are loath to over-lever themselves; and the success of the three banks here demonstrates that slow, steady, and solid growth is the correct strategy to adapt. It may not be sexy, but it is an effective and sound strategy that yields long-term results for shareholders.

Always Remember That You Are Bankers

A fundamental mistake and flawed strategy that the major firms on Wall Street committed was that the CEOs and senior managers stopped thinking of themselves as "bankers" and began to think of themselves as "moneymen" or "financiers." Big mistake. The fundamentals of money and banking never change. Human nature never changes. Once you stop thinking of yourself as a banker, bad things begin to happen. In the community banking world, most

CEOs think of themselves as bankers first and act on the fundamental principles of banking.

The eight fundamental strategies mentioned previously may seem simple and common sense; and they are. However, every one of these "simple" banking strategies were violated by many of the major banking and investment houses on Wall Street and were never followed by many non-bank financial services providers. These strategies are vital to the success of the banks I spoke about.

It's important in this new economy to stick to a formula that will keep you focused to the goals at hand. No matter what the challenge, if you are true to your core principles, your foundation for success will be strong.

16

Donald Marron

Private equity investor and entrepreneur Donald Marron has had his hand in the financial services arena since 1951. Donald is most noted for his role as chairman and CEO of PaineWebber Group from 1980 to 2000. In 2000, Donald was the dealmaker behind PaineWebber's merger with UBS AG, which created the world's top asset management firm. Today, he is thriving in the new economy with his private equity firm, Lightyear Capital, which he co-founded with his managing partner Mark Vassallo. Specializing in financial services companies, Lightyear Capital focuses on leveraged buyouts as well as making growth capital investments in financial services

(*continued*)

(*continued*)
companies. In late spring of 2009, Lightyear Capital was part of a buyout consortium that invested a total of $800 million to acquire South Florida–based bank First Southern. In November of 2009, Marron dove back into the brokerage business with the acquisition of the ING Advisors network and three of ING Advisor Networks five broker-dealers (Financial Network Investment Corporation, Multi-Financial Securities Corporation, and PrimeVest Financial Services). Marron says it was a great investment for Lightyear, adding he sees great opportunity for the three firms as more customers and advisors migrate toward smaller, more nimble, and personalized brokerage firms in the new economy.

Marron is an old-school businessman. He does not discuss deals until they are officially done, a rarity in an age during which private equity firms leak possible deals to the media only to see the deal blow up. It's that standard and philosophy that makes Marron a legend in the financial services arena, and that make his point of view and advice so very valuable.

When I first heard about Bear Stearns, I was in Berlin with my family, which includes two small children (then 12 and 13). I was sitting there watching television, most of which was in German. I immediately thought that this was a seminal event, and here I was out of the United States, relying more on secondhand communication, really just bits and pieces. It was, therefore, difficult for me to sense the full scale of what was going on. However, it did help me to understand what the rest of the world might be experiencing under those circumstances. I did think it was a game-changing event, so much so that I felt for our resources. We had to make sure that they were redeployed in the strongest hands.

We immediately began to assess whether Bear Stearns' failure was an isolated event or if this was the beginning of a chain reaction. In order to determine that, we also had to assess what role private industry would play and what role the government would play. One great comparison I heard was when the first bid was agreed to by J.P. Morgan: two dollars a share to buy Bear Stearns was that the bid was slightly more than the Yankees had paid A-Rod. So you look at that and say, "Okay, that's a private rescue; that's fairly logical." And then you realize no, the government was involved in a big way, providing the $29 billion non-recourse loan to J.P. Morgan to cover possible losses on Bear Stearns' less liquid assets. So you had to ask yourself, "Where will it go?"

Bear Stearns was rescued not because it was too big to fail but rather because it was too *interconnected* to fail; a standard many think should have been applied to Lehman Brothers. And the effects of the acquisition were wide ranging. Clearly, Bear Stearns was a correspondent business that had networks and relationships, in prime brokerage, fixed income, and the commercial real estate market.

Advising Clients

Our clients were interested in knowing as much as they could know about what was happening and why. It became fairly clear that the housing market, which had driven many of these things, was now a big contributor to this. You could see this in securitizations—which led to the greater questions of: Who owned these things? Why did they own them? What were they going to do with them? And how was it going to work? So we were in touch with all of our investors and many of our companies. The second thing we did was raise the question of what kind of portfolios you should have in your own companies. We own several insurance and casualty companies, so one of the things we did immediately was assess their portfolios and get them even more liquid.

Fall of Lehman Brothers

A lot of people share the view that the fall of Lehman Brothers was truly a big shock. First of all, there was a lot of confidence in Lehman Brothers' CEO Dick Fuld; he was seen as a very able manager who had built the company into the powerhouse it was. Second, there were many weeks of speculation about whether Lehman Brothers was going to be sold or take in a large sovereign wealth investment. Deep down, Fuld probably thought nothing worse than a forced sale was going to happen. Finally, there was shock about the *way* Lehman Brothers' failure finally occurred. Right up until that weekend, many assumed that the government would have to step in—not for the sake of Lehman Brothers itself, but because like Bear Stearns, it was linked to many other financial institutions, both in this country and around the world. When the government did not step in, the Law of Unintended Consequences took over.

United States Seizes Control of AIG

The AIG shock was equally big—if not bigger—than Lehman Brothers' bankruptcy. AIG had a reputation as an extraordinary firm under CEO Hank Greenberg's leadership. This was a truly global firm, with some of its origins in China. AIG touched tens of millions of people in the United States. The most ironic part about its fall was that its main business, insurance, inherently *assumes* stability. Insurance basically means that failure won't happen; and even if it does, you will be protected. And here was the nation's leading insurance company—seen by many people as the leading assessor of risk—falling to pieces.

The government's seizure of AIG didn't impact Lightyear's portfolio directly, but we own several companies (albeit much smaller than AIG) that were in the property and casualty business. AIG was such a big player that we immediately started asking ourselves and our companies to understand what the competitive landscape would look like without AIG, and if we were positioned well.

All of AIG's problems raised the fundamental issue of the value of guarantees, insurance, and credit default swaps. We all knew that the growth in credit default swaps was outstripping growth in any other area of financial products, and many of us questioned what the eventual impact would be. AIG's failure to deal with the weight of its credit default swaps demonstrated to the world for the first time what impact these contracts could have on a big company. It put all organizations that held these products on alert.

A Crisis Like No Other

Crises in the financial services industry, where I have been involved for my entire career, happen periodically; and although they never look the same, they usually have the same impact. However, this crisis was different. Most of the prior crises were more or less led by the stock market. This one was the first fixed-income and credit crisis on a global basis. One of the principal factors that accelerated and intensified this crisis was the fact that many of these supposedly liquid assets packaged by the banks and bought by investors throughout the world were in fact *illiquid*. Securitization of retail mortgages had become a very attractive investment product for investors. As a result, banks found increasing incentives and pressure to generate mortgages more and more quickly.

Banks went from thinking of loans not as 30-year loans but as 45- to 60-day loans, and they were holding them just long enough for them to be securitized and sold. In some cases, this resulted in lower lending standards and lower credit standards, as they focused more intensely on high-margin securitization revenue. Of course, the day came when buyers were not interested in these products, and the banks were forced to keep the loans. The whole issue of liquid securities (whole mortgages) becoming illiquid securities (mortgage-backed securities) contributed substantially to the crisis.

This situation was exacerbated by the fact that the rating agencies had assigned triple-A ratings to most of these securitizations. Ultimately, we discovered that even the rating agencies did not really fully understand the construction of these securities, nor were they able to measure the inherent value of liquidity.

Wall Street, which was built over the past 100 years on the premise of making illiquid assets liquid, had finally found a way to make liquid assets illiquid. Mortgages on their own were highly salable; mortgages packaged into securitization became virtually unsalable toxic assets.

Seizing Opportunity

After we made an investment in Lloyd's-based insurance company Antares in late 2007, our investment committee began discussing the investment and operating risks that we and our portfolio companies would face in the coming year. Once we felt comfortable that we were protected in the coming environment and had made sure that the portfolios of our insurance companies were liquid, we carefully began reviewing new investment opportunities. Our early conclusion was that the crisis was yet to play out to its full extent and that given the Law of Unintended Consequences, it would be very hard to predict how broad the impact would be or how long it would last. Therefore, we concluded that we should look at as many opportunities as possible but make no investments unless they were especially compelling. Among the opportunities we were reviewing, the banking industry stood out as an area of real interest.

In this context, we made only one investment in a company called Higher One, which processes the proceeds of student loans. Higher One is a very high growth company and has been relatively unaffected by the crisis. We did, however, use the situation to study opportunities in insurance, banking, and money management, thinking that each of these areas would be affected by this crisis—and in some of these cases, might even provide good opportunities.

One of the first things Lightyear did was assess the investing opportunities in the banking industry. Early in 2008, our investment committee decided that in order to take advantage of these opportunities, Lightyear needed to assign a team of partners to fully understand the landscape and the risks within the banking system. So they got to work by calling more than 200 banks and meeting with the managements of over 100 banks. It was a very interesting exercise, not just because of the deal possibilities, but because it gave us the chance to learn more about what was important to bankers and what was important to their clients. It gave us more information and put us in a good position to act when we felt the time was right.

In our first meetings in late 2007 and early 2008 with the managements, we found most of them saying that they really didn't think they were going to be affected by the situation and that they were not interested in seeking additional capital. Although we didn't agree with this, we believed that we simply had to bide our time. Then, as the crisis unfolded in September and October 2008, the banks began to believe that they might need capital, but they thought they could obtain it from the government (Troubled Asset Relief Program [TARP]) and get it cheaper and perhaps even more easily than they could from private equity. Then months later, they began to think that maybe taking money from the government wasn't such a good idea after all. Finally, they decided that they did need private capital.

This came a year after the United States and other countries began feeling, incrementally, the impact of this crisis: the drastic swings in the stock and bond markets, reduction in the availability of credit, decline in the price of houses, and growing unemployment. So the impact on these community and local banks mirrored what was occurring throughout the country.

In fact, we announced our first bank deal in May 2009. Lightyear and two other firms would be the major investors in an $800 million infusion into a Florida bank called First Southern. This is essentially a small, relatively healthy bank that we believe will serve as a platform for rapid growth through the acquisition of the assets and deposits of troubled banks in Florida.

There will be big opportunities in the financial services industry that are a direct result of this crisis. In private equity, transactions will not be done as a result of leverage or financial engineering this time around. Instead, you'll see private equity focusing more on cost controls, growth opportunities, and operational improvements. Management leverage will replace financial leverage.

Investment Landscape

As I said earlier, there are at least three major areas in financial services that are important to the economy (and to businesses and consumers)—all of which have gone through serious problems: banks, insurance companies, and asset managers.

Banks, are the highest profile and clearly have been the major focus of the past and current administrations. They will be directly affected the most by the regulatory changes that are being proposed. There are more than 8,000 banks in the United States, many more per capita than in any country in the world. Most of these banks are, in fact, healthy, but all of them are impacted by recent events. From our point of view, all this information about the banking system pointed out one central thought—community and local banks now serve an even more important purpose: making loans to buy houses and making loans to small businesses in their communities. In both cases, funds for these loans were drastically reduced; even today we have no indication that credit has loosened up enough to meet the demands that are necessary for consumers and businesses. There is a big opportunity to provide additional capital to these banks to meet the demands to make good loans in both areas.

The second area is insurance. As I said, AIG had a big impact on the insurance industry. The insurance model, particularly in the property and casualty business, is based on writing insurance in a profitable way and successfully investing the capital they get from the insurance premiums. Both of these areas were hard hit in 2008. On the liability side, companies were hit by two devastating hurricanes: Ike and Gustav. And, of course, their portfolios experienced substantial declines in the stock and fixed-income markets. Nonetheless, many of these businesses (including ours) were strong, solid businesses that provide essential services. We see real opportunities here, partly because rates are starting to go up due to the reduced available capital in the industry and partly because there is increased technology that is available to manage risk. We currently own parts of four insurance companies, and we may consider additional opportunities.

The third area is asset management. With the stock market down as much as 30 to 40 percent and fixed-income markets in disarray, most asset managers have seen substantial declines in the value of their portfolios. After the events of 2008, clients routinely open their statements to find 30 to 50 percent reductions in their equity portfolios. College endowments and pensions saw declines of 25 to 40 percent. This, of course, has had a big impact on the life of individuals and institutions. Colleges have had to cut back spending and had bond issues because of the lack of liquidity in the markets; pension plan managers have had concerns about how they are going to meet their payments; and individuals have lost substantial amounts of money.

Individuals in particular have felt this more than any prior crisis, because this has been the first 401(k) crisis. We live in a world of 50 million self-administered pension plan managers. So rather than just being spectators or indirectly affected, individuals have been directly affected and are postponing retirement, rethinking lifestyles, and cutting spending altogether. This means there is an important opportunity in asset management. The creditability of asset managers is at a new low, but the necessity for their services is, in many ways, at a new high. All financial assets have to and are now going to be managed in the context of this crash.

Transparency and Restructuring Positives

Obviously, this kind of financial crisis is going to stimulate new regulation. In fact, as of this writing, the president has proposed an extensive overhaul of how banks, insurance companies, and other financial service companies and their products are currently regulated. I hope the three main principles are embodied in the debate. First, in terms of investing, it is essential that we have transparency. If you know what you are buying and what you are selling, and you know what you are managing, then you can do well. This kind of transparency was missing, particularly in terms of securitization. Second, we need to somehow limit the degree of complexity of securitized products and derivatives. Third, to ensure that investors regain confidence in these institutions, we need to make sure that the issuers and the market makers of the securities are properly capitalized to cover their positions and restrain them from taking on excessive leverage. Specific proposals should therefore include requirements that: (1) issuers of securitizations hold at least 5 percent in their own account of each security they package and sell; (2) market makers in derivatives have enough liquid capital (much more than today) to have a cushion from what they are doing; and (3) complex financial products are standardized so that they can be listed on exchanges.

Lay of the Economic Land

Beginning at the end of the first quarter of 2009, the underlying economic environment was experiencing improvements. A big part of the stock market recovery stems from the fact that we know more because we have more tools. A good example is the stress test on the banks. You can question whether they were tough enough, but what is definite is that the world now knows a lot more about these banks than they ever knew before, and there is real value in this. Transparency will give investors more confidence in the system, even if it doesn't give them more incentive to invest right now.

The consumer drives the American economy, and the average American consumer is very smart. Having run PaineWebber and seeing consumers in action, I'm not sure they've been given enough credit. At the beginning of this crisis in August and September, the consumers decided something was wrong, stopped spending, and started saving. They cut spending by 20 to 25 percent, pushing the savings rates from nothing to 4 to 5 percent.

Is that a fundamental change in the trend? Or is this just a savvy reaction to difficulties now supplanted by different worries such as unemployment and housing values, and then down the road of the fear of inflation? I am an optimist, so I think we will work our way out of this and return to a 3 to 4 percent growth rate. But it could very well be two or three years before that happens, and it is going to feel like a long two or three years. So much of the recovery depends on the confidence of Americans, and the president has a big role to play in that.

So what has changed? Investors, businesspeople, and consumers have gone from worrying about disaster to assessing the present and the future. The analysis of the bank has gone from, "Will this bank be in business next year?" to "How much can this bank earn in this climate?" Consumers and investors who were originally feeling they had to have all their money in cash or gold are now once again considering investing, but very cautiously.

You cannot solve a housing crisis until you get buyers, and we don't really have enough programs to stimulate buyers yet. Ultimately, we need credit. I believe we will start to see credit become available by the end of 2009.

Bottom Line

We need to address the three issues in order to solve this crisis. The first is that although the government has saved the banks, it hasn't fixed them yet. Second, the housing crisis got us into this, and solving it will get us out of it. Third, since the consumer drives the American economy, there has to be a constructive return of confidence and willingness to commit.

These issues need to be confronted simultaneously. More importantly, the president's stimulus plan and the Federal Reserve's fiscal and monetary policies have to be seen as actually affecting individuals. We will see the effects actually working when the consumers say, "Yes, that plan helped me to buy this house" (or get this job or get a student loan for my kids). There is not a lot of that yet, but it is in its early days.

This environment has created a whole new world of possibilities. The American spirit of optimism will prevail.

Part Three

Real Estate

17

Richard LeFrak

The boom and catastrophic bust of the real estate market will be studied by business minds for years to come. Now we are faced with another crisis: the lack of funding for commercial loans. One of my favorite real estate contacts that's in both residential and commercial real estate is Richard LeFrak, chairman and CEO of the LeFrak Organization. Richard is facing headwinds from two sides, and is able to navigate around the challenges and see opportunities to grow his portfolio.

(*continued*)

(*continued*)

Richard LeFrak comes from a dynasty of entrepreneurs. His grandfather Harry originally created glassworks for Louis Comfort Tiffany, and in the early 1900s, he began developing New York City real estate. Soon after World War II, Richard's father, Sam, began developing the company further by building apartment houses throughout New York City and New Jersey. In 1959, he began developing LeFrak City in Queens, a vast complex of 5,000 apartments in twenty 18-story buildings on 42 acres of land along the Long Island Expressway.

In the 1970s, Richard joined the family business. Soon, under his supervision, the company began developing the 92-acre Manhattan landfill to be known as Battery Park City and building its first 1,700 luxury apartments. Since the mid-1980s, the LeFrak Organization has been developing Newport, the largest and most successful waterfront community in the United States, on several hundred acres on the Jersey City bank of the Hudson River. To date, more than 15 million square feet have been completed, along with apartments for approximately 5,000 families, office space for more than 20,000 employees, shopping facilities for more than 2 million annual visitors, two major hotels, a marina, parks, schools, and even an ice-skating rink.

Richard is more than just a New York area developer and builder. The LeFrak portfolio includes a worldwide range of financial investments, real estate in Los Angeles and London, and interests in oil and gas wells, as well as wind energy production. LeFrak made news in May 2009, when the investing group that he was a part of became owners of the Florida bank BankUnited, which was seized by the Federal Deposit Insurance Corporation (FDIC). The group put up $900 million in new capital into the failed bank, which got dragged down in the real estate undertow.

Richard is a natural when it comes to interviews, which is ironic considering that he never really "did TV" until he appeared on my show. I knew from my first pre-interview that he would be great, and to this day, he has never disappointed our viewers. He has the ability to connect with people because he can break down a complex situation into a story that people can relate to. His stories often are harbingers of things to come.

My story of the market meltdown actually takes me back to August 2007 with an anecdote that, in hindsight, should have been the first indication of what our industry and the nation might be facing. It was a clue that was so obvious that I should have realized what was about to happen, even if the reality would be difficult to accept.

I'm a member of a Long Island golf club where there's a caddie who we'll call "Jimmy" for the sake of anonymity. He's in his early 50s, has 14 or 15 children, and makes his living full time as a caddie. I would help him out from time to time if he was having money problems. Sometime in late summer 2007, Jimmy came to me and said, "Mr. LeFrak, I have a great opportunity to buy a house." I asked him where the house was, and he said in the Bronx. He then wanted me to consider lending him $5,000 for a down payment. I asked Jimmy how much the house would cost. He said $800,000. A bit startled, I asked, "Where would you get the money to do that?" Given his circumstances, it sounded like a large amount of money for somebody who would not have the down payment or income necessary to purchase an $800,000 home. His answer was that the broker who was selling him the house reassured him that he could get him a mortgage.

This was a graphic example of the aggressive nature of the subprime mortgage market at that time, and I should have realized that it might be leading to a giant financial downfall. I should have acted by selling everything I owned, because it was a clear signal that we had really gone over the edge in terms of how we were allocating credit.

The following year, in 2008, there were a number of very highly priced transactions in the real estate business, including the purchase of Equity Office Properties and Stuyvesant Town. Both were multibillion dollar deals accomplished with an enormous amount of leverage. Again, these were clear signals that reality had escaped the credit markets. As long as you could come up with any idea, there was someone to lend you money to achieve it. After having been in the business for so many years, I should instinctively have been aware of this mushrooming dilemma. Did I act as I should have? No, I did not. We did sell a portfolio of buildings in 2007 and 2008, something we rarely do. But, in hindsight, I realize I didn't do as much as I should have to take advantage of the leverage mania.

Putting a Strategy Together Post–Lehman Brothers

It's also ironic that Lehman Brothers went under a few days after I appeared on CNBC's *Squawk Box* on September 11 with my dear friend, and former head of Shearson Lehman, Peter Cohen. The subject of Lehman Brothers' solvency was discussed on the air that day, because everybody was concerned about the firm's ability to survive. Unfortunately, Lehman Brothers didn't make it. In retrospect, that too was probably the biggest mistake that the financial regulators made—letting Lehman Brothers go under—because the credit markets obviously froze up; the panic set in, and we crept toward the edge of the abyss of the financial system as we had known it. My reaction after that terrible event was to take stock of my company's assets and to try to find out where all our cash was. Who was holding it? What were our short-term investments? We tried to identify, reorganize, and put our cash in extremely safe instruments.

Everyone in my company's financial department—controller, treasurer, and chief investment officer—was told to catalog explicitly not only how the money was invested but who was holding it and how it was being held; for example, in what street name or in what custody accounts? And where were these custody accounts? Although we didn't panic, there was a sense of urgency, and that process took several weeks to complete.

Managing Through the Credit Crisis

When the credit crisis emerged, I thought that I would have to reserve my liquidity for my business to pay down loans as they came due. I did not believe that banks, with their restricted balance sheets, would be in a position to refinance existing amounts of many loans. I always keep a conservative loan book; that's one of the reasons why we've been able to stay in business as long as we have. We always believe that loans have to amortize. I don't believe in standing loans that just pay interest. I never did any securitized financing. I always want to be able to look my lender in the eye, especially if I have any problems. My loans were made through insurance companies, banks, and pension funds. Still, we were very careful with scheduling our liabilities to make sure that as loans came due (and fortunately, we didn't have very much happening in 2009), we would have the liquidity to pay them down to a level to keep banks happy. In real property finance, you have to differentiate between commercial and multifamily residential assets.

The Commercial Apartment House Financing market is the beneficiary of Fannie Mae and Freddie Mac government credit support. An active financing market is available in apartment house product, as long as it fits within their criteria, and most of our residential properties fit within that envelope. On the other hand, offices, retail space, and hotels do not have the benefit of

Fannie Mae or Freddie Mac. Those are situations where we must deal with traditional lenders or securitized loans. Securitized loans, for all intents and purposes, ceased at the end of 2008, creating an acute need for capital. At this point, capital and the structure for dispersing capital virtually do not exist.

I always took loans that are highly conservative by the standards of other real estate companies. That also meant that I was not as aggressive as other people who had been participating in the bubble of leverage during the past five years.

Assessing Liabilities and Creating Opportunities

Right after the bubble burst, we immediately reviewed the liability side of our balance sheet. We asked ourselves what obligations we faced and how we would cover them. Cash would have to be available in case we were challenged. Once we realized the problem was passing—and we had sufficient working capital and cash in the business—we began focusing on what we were prepared to do next in the market. I was particularly concerned because although we've coped with downturns in the past, none had ever been quite as formidable as this. We faced problems in 1973, 1974, in the early 1980s and early 1990s, when the real estate business had been severely affected. There would be the inevitable impact on general market demand; rent rolls and cash flow would suffer. I knew that I would have to make up for that.

So we invested our free cash in a way that ensured that we would have sufficient reserves to support the core business. I began studying opportunities that were becoming available. For a while, high rates of return were available through reasonably safe debt instruments. Members of my staff were busy investigating the many opportunities presented to them. Then they would meet with me or my two sons, Harrison and Jamie, on a regular basis to discuss potential investments. Sometime in late October or early November, when yields on municipals had reached high levels, we decided that we would invest in some long-term, high-quality bonds. We invested several hundred millions of dollars in these instruments, which we determined to be substantially safe.

The rationale for the investment was quite simple. Yields on some tax-free investments had reached 7 to 8 percent per annum, which equaled 14 to 16 percent on comparable taxable bonds. Many of these bonds were backed by the federal government, as they were issued by the Federal National Mortgage Association (FNMA) or Freddie Mac, which by that time had been taken over by the federal government. Other bonds were backed by secure streams of income with dedicated water, sewer, or sales tax revenue. We believed that at that level of return, the limited risk was justified.

Optimist at Heart

Keep in mind that I'm a builder by trade; and a builder is always by nature an optimist. This is the first time in 15 years that I don't have a new building underway. But I have been expanding my business in other very sound and conservative ways, such as my recent investment in BankUnited.

Historically, I always constructed only a few buildings at a time. As I'd finish one and finance it conservatively, I would start another. Since April of 2009, I've completed a 430-room Westin Hotel; 400 condominium units; an office building in Los Angeles; and a 360-unit luxury rental apartment tower in New Jersey. It's not that I'm out of business. But if you asked me what I might have on the agenda for 2010, the answer is that I'm using my capital to make investments in either existing assets (finished real properties) or in other asset classes, such as BankUnited in Florida.

"Bad Bank" Opportunity

I recently participated in the investor group of a failed bank in Florida called BankUnited. This institution had significant assets tied up in subprime and exotic mortgage paper, associated with the big real estate bust in Florida. BankUnited had more than $8 billion in deposits and $10.5 billion in assets, many of which were in arrears and not worth a mere fraction of their face value.

We were invited to bid on the failing bank with former North Fork Bank CEO John Kanas and Wilbur Ross. John had great success with North Fork and had a terrific management team that was prepared to take on this challenge. Despite all the problems in Florida, I believe the state has a tremendous future because of the country's demographics. Many of the post-war generation are starting to retire and will be attracted to Florida by the low tax environment and sunshine. A well-run bank in Florida should succeed; and John Kanas and his team were the right people to lead it.

We participated in a complex bidding process that required us to recapitalize the bank with more than $900 million and agree on a loss sharing formula with federal regulators. By buying the franchise, the branches, and deposits, and putting in the money to make the bank an extremely well capitalized institution, John and his team have a running head start. I expect this investment to make an outstanding return. Moreover, this gives us a platform to buy other failing institutions in our primary market and turn this bank into a much larger institution.

Investing in "Toxic" Assets

There are opportunities in real estate to invest in loans that, although often inaccurately called toxic, are simply mispriced. In many instances, these assets are "toxic" only because the banks hold a mark-to-market value on their books that is much higher than the assets' true market value. Nevertheless, they're not without value; even a lemon has a price. But these assets have to be bought at the right price and studied and evaluated with great precision. At the end, if investors are wise and meticulous and have done their due diligence, there will be a reasonable rate of return—perhaps 20 to 30 percent for the risk involved—because those investors have done their homework.

There will be some excellent opportunities to invest in real estate in the future. Both debt and equity markets have been fractured by the failure in capital markets. A severe recession, during which rents are falling while vacancy rates increase, is compounding the problem and leaving cash flows uncertain. Moreover, the mania that produced cap rates of 4 to 5 percent for properties has been replaced by a far more sober environment. A few properties that have traded have seen price declines of as much as 60 percent. In some cases, sales have been accomplished only with seller financing. In the end, buying property below its replacement cost with conservative judgments about rents will lead to very positive returns.

The year 2010 will present many opportunities for those who have the cash to take advantage of them. For small investors, the real estate investment trusts (REITs) may prove to be a good space in which to invest if the companies have good assets, strong balance sheets, and solid management, and they operate in strong and growing markets.

The Black Swan event has taken place in real estate, and when the prices adjust, the future will be excellent. We are starting to look in New York and Los Angeles—our primary markets of interest—for properties that conform to these standards.

Thriving Strategies

To thrive in this new economy, you must have a clear picture of what to expect from people. You need to reassure them that you have given enough forethought to what bad times can mean and that your business will be able to survive in those bad times. You must be concerned about employees and their fears because many of them are apprehensive about job security. You can't be negative. If you're a pessimist, don't go into business, because success won't be in your future. In the end, business relies on two things: capital and human capital. And you must keep the human capital motivated.

18

Don Peebles

Prominent real estate developer Don Peebles has been around hotels his entire life and is often referred to as the "African American Donald Trump." Peebles's grandfather was a doorman for 41 years at the Marriott Wardman Park Hotel in Washington, DC, and his mother ran a successful real estate firm. Don himself runs one of the country's largest minority-owned real estate development companies, with a net worth of $350 million. His portfolio includes The Royal Palm Hotel and The Lincoln in Miami Beach, Florida, and Washington's Courtyard by Marriott Convention Center.

Don's ability to be flexible in turbulent market conditions is one of his greatest assets. In 2007, he purchased 13 acres in Las Vegas for $65 million, with the intention of developing a luxury resort hotel and condominium on the same lot

(*continued*)

(*continued*)
of an existing apartment building. But then the real estate market collapsed in Vegas, and funding for projects was nowhere to be found. Don instead looked at the money that his apartment tenants were bringing in as a way to generate income during the downturn, and he has decided to wait for now to start his project. Don's ability to be nimble is the key to his success in thriving in the new economy.

At that point in time (in September 2008), there were banks and institutions that most people assumed would never have failed. But history can be a guide for the future. After all, in the early 1990s, large banking institutions that had been around for decades were failing. So based on the events of September, 2008, we were now going to see some significant distress in the market. It happened very quickly, probably more so than I would've expected. But it wasn't a big surprise. We eventually saw credit freeze up, especially on the real estate side. History was beginning to repeat itself—and I saw it as a potential opportunity. I knew what was going to happen; people were going to panic.

In real estate or the stock market, the air has to inevitably be let out of the balloon for people to make money again, because at a certain point, you can't keep making money in a continuously rising market—it becomes too competitive. In my business, there are no real opportunities to get value on the buy side when there is a line of people who are willing to pay more than the next person. That is one of the biggest challenges in the boom market.

In some regards, I was surprised by what happened. But I was also excited, because although it was sad that people were going to be losing a lot of money, there were now going to be opportunities that would come from it. I viewed it as though we were entering into a different market cycle.

Timing Your Opportunity

When I look at a market cycle, I use a clock as a gauge. That is, 12 o'clock is the peak, and 6 o'clock is the dip. We went from 12 o'clock to 4 o'clock exceptionally quickly. In September 2008, the credit freeze brought us to about 4 o'clock, but it didn't bring us to the worst yet. We are now over the peak, and we're on our way down to 6 o'clock.

I have always regarded real estate as a cyclical business, and this is the time to begin gearing up to take advantage of the opportunities. I consider several aspects when I evaluate any real estate opportunity. No matter what, it's always important to buy quality. In a rapidly rising market, quality is essentially unaffordable in terms of making good returns. So in order to buy quality, you have to settle for subpar returns. That makes it far more of an institutional environment as opposed to an entrepreneurial environment. However, during a recession—and a dramatic downturn in the marketplace where fundamentals are out of whack—quality becomes accessible and affordable. We, therefore, look to buy quality and take advantage of the market dysfunction. I saw the value of quality assets going down quickly and significantly, which we perceived as a prospect.

In addition to buying quality, we also look to deal directly with the parties. We're not interested in engaging in a broad competition, bidding with thousands of other people for troubled bank assets, or going out on a bidding contest. We're looking to find opportunities where we can buy quality at significant discounts. And we're also looking at discounts where the values are at their peaks, somewhere between $0.50 and $0.75 on the dollar. We want to buy assets from 25 percent to approximately 40 percent of what their peak value was. That normally brings us back to a valuation that more closely resembles the beginning of the rise in values after the mid-1990s pullback. We seek to buy quality at depressed prices and for fundamental distress—which in the credit market, involves more owners' distress.

Location, Location, Location

We are also, of course, looking for geographic qualities. I always consider major markets that have a great deal of attraction, and there are a handful of these for which we have an appetite: the Washington, DC, metropolitan area; the New York metropolitan area, mainly New York City; San Francisco; Los Angeles; Las Vegas; and to a lesser degree, South Florida and the Chicago area. These locations are world-class international cities with strong underlying fundamentals that have been hurt by the global meltdown. We are then looking for premier locations within those premier cities.

After we get the location, the third element we consider is—if it's an existing property—the level of quality in terms of design and physical structure of the building. A great example of this was the development of my first hotel, The Royal Palm. I heard about it on a visit to Miami Beach, during which I read a newspaper article about the city's desire to redevelop The Royal Palm Hotel—and the opportunity intrigued me. Getting fully developed sites generally requires the assembling of properties, something that was new to people in Miami, but not to me. I went out and bought the hotel next door to The Royal Palm Hotel—which I planned to use for expansion—and then bid for the city site, which was The Royal Palm Hotel. I bid against local developers and prominent families, and even hotel chain giants like Ritz-Carlton and Hyatt. And I was able to win because I understood the value of site control of the neighboring property, which was a necessity to redevelop The Royal Palm Hotel property.*

The idea is not to chase the market, and to try to buy value. Of course, it's a lot easier to buy value in a down market, and it is much more challenging to do in an up market. Most often, you'll have to procure value the way that I did with The Royal Palm—through a public-private partnership.

---

* *Author's note:* Site control is when you have the legal right to use a piece of land. Leases, deeds, and easements are examples of site control.

Another method is the one that we used to secure the site that we built with the American Psychological Association. It was an amazing opportunity for us, because the price of that land was set so low that we were able to pay off the other developer at cost. It was a win-win situation; they got out of a failed project without losing any money, and we bought the land still significantly below market and turned an amazing profit. We were able to do this because, unlike the previous developer, we had a tenant for the building, and the tenant—the American Psychological Association—was able to use tax-exempt status to obtain certificates of participation (which was a precursor to the CMBS market[†]).

Not Abandoning Old Strategies

In the past, I used this strategy out of necessity; when I was building my company, I couldn't afford to have a big loss. Therefore, I had to be very conservative and build brick by brick while simultaneously relying on high leverage and well-above-market returns. I started my business with no money. I had a couple of challenges that I needed to confront. One of these was that I wanted to create some significant wealth, and I wanted to do it in a short time period. Real estate traditionally has a longer-term investment period of 5 to 10 years.

One of the things that I tried to do as I faced the obstacle of building a business with no money was to use leverage, which is a difficult and risky thing to do in a rising market. So the best time to use leverage is in a down market.

Building from Nothing

When I first started my company in the mid-1980s, Washington, DC politics were focused on rebuilding neighborhoods—because

[†] *Author's note:* A CMBS is a commercial backed mortgage security. These are securities that are backed by commercial properties.

that's where the voters lived. I was able to capitalize on the desire for the city to create urban redevelopment and present a proposition: a public-private partnership in developing a site where I would build in a declining area that would jump-start the revitalizing process.

I learned a lot about the political process when I attended the Capitol Page School at the Library of Congress, where I was an intern for two years and worked for Representatives Conyers and Dellums. The relationships I forged during that time helped me navigate my way through local DC politics. I eventually chaired DC's tax appeals board. My knowledge of working my way around the political process was helpful in getting regulatory approval.

I found a site in Anacostia on Martin Luther King Avenue, an area that had once been an economically thriving corridor but had recently declined. Since there was a desire to redevelop it, I approached the city to get them to lease the office space on that corridor. I had an edge: First, I found the site. Second, I had the tenant, and I could pay very little for the site. The building I ultimately built was a 100,000-square-foot building, which is considered a medium-sized office building in Washington, DC. That land downtown would have cost me between $10 million and $15 million in that time in the marketplace. Instead, I was able to buy it for $900,000. I then went to investors and presented them with a proposition. They could own 50 percent of an office building fully leased to the government, and they put up all the money. I delivered the government and the site. The risk of developing an office building comes in the form of leasing risk if you build it on spec.

But since I had a tenant in hand, that took risk out of the equation. The only question that was left was how to execute the construction. If it was done in a timely manner, then the government was obligated to take the space. They were a credit tenant, one of the best in the area. As a result, I hired a general contractor to do a design build, thus taking the risk of design and completion away from the developer and putting it in the design builder contractor's hands. We made an agreement that essentially said, "Here is a building; you can deliver it to me within _____ amount of time, at a guaranteed maximum price." As a result, that was my first deal.

Once that building was constructed, it provided me with an income of $300,000 to $400,000 a year. It started with development fees once we broke ground, and then went on to an income stream. I still own that building today, almost 20 years after I delivered it.

And that is the strategy we still use today. We have never changed our underwriting purchasing philosophy; this has put us in a position where we can do well. In real estate, you make your money when you buy; you realize your profit when you sell. But to make that profit, you earn it when you buy.

Unfortunately, a lot of people think they understand how that works. People who buy never expect the hot market to end, especially on their watch. They figure that they can play the game of musical chairs, and when the music stops, they're going to have a seat. No one expects bad things to happen to them. The same is true of a tragic car accident or a terminal disease, but these things *do* happen to some people. When money is the issue, we all ought to expect bad things to happen. We *must* plan for them. I can plan (somewhat) for the unexpected when I drive home by buckling my seat belt, driving carefully, and not drinking before I take the wheel. That's the best I can do. I can mitigate my risk in business by being disciplined with my underwriting.

So we look to discipline ourselves. We want to make the strongest return with a qualified risk, one that we are comfortable taking and one whose risk we believe we can mitigate. That makes it unique for us. We happen to be comfortable going through the political process, so we can take a land-use entitlement risk because we understand that risk.

It's All About Timing

One of the biggest misunderstandings among investors is their assumption that they have to wait to buy real estate at the "bottom."

Although timing is important, it's important for investors to recognize that they can't buy at the *absolute* bottom, because what's left at that point are lesser-quality products. And when purchasing real estate, you've got to find the best-quality assets at the best opportunities. Let the *opportunities* dictate when you buy. Although we may be at only 4:00 or 4:30 on our clock, perhaps the seller is desperate and is actually selling the property at 6 o'clock prices out of need. Real estate must be evaluated on a case-by-case basis. Anybody who says, "Now is not the time to buy," is making an overall sector decision, as opposed to considering specific assets. We are an entrepreneurial company, so if a certain benefit makes a good buy, then we will buy it. Values on the whole may have a statistical basis to go down, but there are some properties that are already depressed sufficiently to buy. And they're not going to go down much lower, because somebody else is going to come and buy them.

Certain factors will give you a sense of whether you're buying at a good price. If you have an understanding of the market and are able to see what kind of immediate income potential the property has, then that's a good sign. Maybe it's an undeveloped parcel of land, so you ask yourself what a finished product would cost today and how it's utilizing that land price. What kind of position would that put you in as a finished product today? Where do you think things are going to stabilize? How far back into the market would that price be (if you're buying something on a value based on, say, 1996 prices)? That tells you there may be an opportunity to buy. If you go back much further than that, the opportunity is not as favorable. It's all risk. What's the end game, and what is the end use for the property on the real estate side? What is your exit to profit?

Challenges on the Horizon

In addition to depressed residential real estate prices, there is another challenge unfolding in my industry—and that's the commercial credit crisis. But again, with every crisis comes opportunities. You have to look at the whole picture. I am seeing great potential for my company, because when there is less available capital and less available financing, prices go down—it really is an all-cash buyer's market. For example, we're now in the process of putting together a billion dollar investment fund for real estate.

This shortage of capital was something I saw in the early 1990s, when the banks were closing and the regulators were pressing the lenders to divest themselves of commercial real estate loans. The lenders at that time were kicking real estate loans off their books, further depressing prices and creating tremendous opportunities. That's initially what prompted the Wall Street private equity funds to go into real estate—there was a void in the marketplace. The traditional real estate debt market had collapsed. What will ultimately happen in this time period is that the markets are going to come up with products that will alleviate this problem. So the money has to be made prior to the early stages of a new approach in financing. Then, everything will run up again. It might take 10 to 15 years to peak again, but it will.

Time Check

Things should stabilize somewhat in 2010, hit the bottom, and then hover there for a while. The good news is that the places that initially led the decline, such as Las Vegas, are bottoming out. In fact, Las Vegas is seeing huge increases in sales volume, primarily because of all the foreclosures and short sales. It's so affordable that it's almost irresistible for people not to buy there now. As prices continue to go down, velocity will pick up on the housing market.

The real challenge is going to be in the job market; it's going to take new industries time to create jobs. Look at the significant job losses in the automobile industry; those are just the beginning. Manufacturing across the board is down considerably. There are also extensive job losses—and more expected—in the financial sector. It will take the economy some time to generate new jobs, something that will be a considerable part of the recovery.

In any kind of business—real estate, entrepreneurial—there are times when the overall economy is good and times when it's bad. But remember that whatever business you're in, you're there for the long term. An entrepreneur needs to be able to make money in all environments. In my profession, when it's a good time to sell, you want to sell. When it's a good time to buy, you want to buy. When it's a good time to study and understand the fundamentals and prospects, then you do that. You're not just in business when it's a good time to sell, or buy, or develop. The challenge is to operate well in every aspect, during every part of the cycle. If you can do that, then you will be successful—because you will be profitable when others aren't.

Another element here is geographic and product-type diversification. In my approach to real estate, for example, that means different types of uses of the property, such as hotel, residential, office, and retail properties. You need to consider geographic diversity as well, something that also allows you to look at different sectors and pick product types that fit certain markets. And if the market rebounds, it puts you in a position of strength, where the only thing that will bring it down is a national or global recession. But even in such a case, you will have a softer landing.

19

Ron Peltier

To get a sense of what's going on in the residential real estate market, I call on Ron Peltier, chairman and CEO of HomeServices of America, a Berkshire Hathaway affiliate. HomeServices of America, which is the second-largest U.S. residential real estate brokerage, expanded its real estate thumbprint in the fall of 2009 when it bought Koenig & Strey GMAC Real Estate for an undisclosed price from Brookfield Residential Property Services. The transaction added 900 additional agents to its sales fleet. Although HomeServices of America avoided the subprime market, that didn't insulate them from the real estate domino effect. However, Ron's new strategies have helped his company survive the housing turmoil.

We saw the real estate market really begin to boom right after the equities market collapsed, in mid-summer 2000, and it continued to pick up momentum. It started in a few states, most specifically California, Arizona, Florida, and Nevada, and quickly expanded to other markets, but it did not hit every market at once, nor did it hit with the same sort of force.

We clearly saw that the market was getting ahead of itself in terms of velocity and rapidly escalating home values. Long-established practices of mortgage models and financing standards gave way to creative low-risk financing. Speculators crept into a mix of business that led them to purchase a primary residence and shift it to an investment vehicle, with the sole motivation to quickly resell or flip properties for profit. While we saw the force of this robust market continue to grow beyond normal real estate cycles, it was difficult to regulate this activity.

Business operators attempted to maintain our market share and scalable business activity and balance that with good business sense. One of the more compelling challenges for us was managing an expansion that we knew in many ways was suspect. During this period, we increased our overhead, our employees, our programs, and our footprint within our respective markets. Although we believe we managed this process better than most, hindsight would tell us that it was not prudent to have expanded to such a large degree.

In retrospect, we would have been better off being satisfied as an organization with slower growth of business activity that was more consistent with what we could reasonably support. Our business rose by about 40 percent above the norm during its peak. Interestingly enough, because of the weight of the crash, it has corrected back down and then slightly more from its norm. Our entire industry has paid the price of expansion and overinvestment in infrastructure. It was a lot more difficult to unwind than it was to build up.

Buildup of Subprime

We have a significant mortgage relationship with Wells Fargo. Although many creative mortgage products exist in the marketplace, Wells Fargo maintained its disciplined mortgage processes and programs and did not participate in this arena. Our sales associates did sell products and homes to customers who ultimately took advantage of these creative products through alternative avenues. There was an abundance of lenders who were aggressively competing for the subprime business and other creative mortgage products, which created a true feeding frenzy.

Unwinding of Credit

The unwinding of credit markets in August and September 2008 was very challenging and painful. The markets simply froze. The ultimate driver that allows the real estate transaction to go from initial contact to closing is the mortgage component. People at all economic levels want to own a home, but the cash side of the transaction is actually a very small piece; this means that having a mortgage product that matches the purchasers' needs is critical.

When Lehman Brothers collapsed and the financial markets seized up, we saw a 180-degree turn in the market from an environment where there were virtually no credit standards and no real price put on risk in the mortgage markets, to a situation where even the most creditworthy people were being shut out. That abrupt shift in our ability to do business was both unnerving and challenging. We experienced an environment where—for five or six years—traditional credit and mortgage underwriting standards continued to erode to a point where the industry had no standards at all. Now, the pendulum has swung too far in the opposite direction, and traditional mortgage lending practices have become more restrictive. It was a very frustrating market, one that caused tremendous pain in the marketplace, not only for customers and clients, but for our sales associates attempting to deliver an unparalleled level of service.

Unwinding in Order to Thrive

Our industry, which grew almost "unnaturally," has shrunk just as dramatically. From our peak, we have closed approximately 100 offices (about 25 percent), eliminated most of the full-time employees who were hired during the growth peak, and downsized our sales force by just under 30 percent, and we are experiencing revenues similar to those of the pre-boom days.

The entire industry grew 40 percent during the boom. This included an increase of sales associates, mortgage officers, title officers, and servicers of property casualty and insurance. It has been a huge adjustment for these individuals, as we all have had to do more with a lot less. When it is all said and done, we were trying to catch a rising star on its way up . . . and we expended a lot of our resources trying to catch it. As the market contracted, and it did so quicker and harder than anyone anticipated, the entire industry was bloodied by the falling sword.

The lesson we learned is that although it is difficult to work through downsizing, we are clearly positioned as an organization for the current market. We are confident that we can be a profitable, effective, and efficient organization in the current environment. We know that the markets will continue to show more activity and strength. We have a better view of the marketplace and the discipline to take more measured actions during fluctuations.

When you are in the real estate business, you establish a perspective about standard industry metrics. The metrics that are associated with our business include growth in total home sales units and home appreciation values. Typically, total home sales units were steady at 3 to 4 percent over a 50- to 75-year historical period, and homes generally appreciate at 4 to 5 percent per year on a national basis.

What we were seeing in this overheated market environment was that home sales activity grew from 5 million existing home sales to about 7.2 million existing home sales from 2000 to 2005, up almost 40 percent.

Additionally, new construction increased from about 800,000 builds to just under 2 million builds per year. All of that speculation created a shortage of inventory; demand outstripped the available supply for each and every build. At the same time, in many markets, home values were appreciating in double digits year after year. Instead of our normal growth of 3 to 5 percent in appreciation, we were seeing home values going up to 12, 15, 18, and 20 percent year-over-year. Sales associates saw this as a huge opportunity to talk to their customers about the purchase transaction as an investment opportunity, in addition to being a place to call home. As a result, we saw people accelerating their natural schedule for buying a home and trading up.

In addition to trading homes more frequently, customer appetite for homes was expanding. Whereas people used to buy just one home, now they were buying in greater numbers than historical averages. About 25 percent of this activity was speculator-driven, meaning that their primary motivation to purchase was to realize the property appreciation and then to resell it at a significantly higher price. It is fair to say that at some point, almost every person in the business believed that this was not sustainable. However, people felt that they were going to take advantage of every opportunity that was out there while it lasted.

Thriving Strategies

Now it's back to the basics. First, we believe that the underlying principles are sound: that real estate, as a primary residence—a place to call home—is desirable for both families and individuals. There is a tremendous desire to own a home, and over a period of time, it is still a solid long-term investment. What we are trying to clearly communicate to our customers and clients is that home ownership is not the type of investment that should be made for a short-term flip. Families and individuals purchasing above their means—and through creative mortgage vehicles that will reset in two or three years and are not sustainable on their current income—are indeed making unwise decisions. It is critical when securing a mortgage in today's environment that they receive proper guidance from knowledgeable professionals.

We are tempering back the enthusiasm of our sales associates as well as consumers about how quickly they can build wealth through real estate. And although I'm one of the proponents of bringing a tempered perspective to home ownership, that encouragement needs to be balanced with the idea that there is underlying value in residential real estate and that over time, purchasing a home is a good investment.

Another thing that we are continuously evaluating is the size of the market, which is currently off 40 percent from its peak. We are educating all of our companies on what we believe is the new norm; in the future, "normal" will be less. I do not believe we will get back to our peak level of approximately 7.2 million existing home sales for another five to seven years.

The postscript is that we have been seeing price destruction, particularly influenced or impacted by the real estate–owned (REO) business. This erosion of value will continue at least through the end of 2009. I do believe we will see stabilization, but probably no appreciation, in home values before 2011.

Silver Lining

We still have significant demand for homeownership in the future. The tax benefits that the Obama administration has put in place (the $8,000 tax credit), in tandem with the historical low interest rates, has led to tremendous pickup in sales activity for the lower-end-priced homes and for first-time home buyers. As a direct result, a tremendous buying opportunity now exists for potential homeowners. Buyers who thought they'd never be in a position to own a home just a couple years ago now have ample selection and affordability at record lows. There *is* a silver lining here; but it is coming at a tremendous price considering the record number of foreclosures. We are currently envisioning approximately 2 million foreclosures for the year coming on the market, and that probably will continue into early 2010.

The impact of all these foreclosures is that we have a bifurcated real estate marketplace. Currently, approximately 50 percent of all sales taking place nationally are distressed, or foreclosure-related. We also have the non-distressed homeowners, whose properties are, for the most part, within 10 to 15 percent of the values attained during the peak of the market; and those sales prices are being driven down by the foreclosures.

But if you are not a seller or in a highly distressed neighborhood, your home value is still relatively secure and solid, particularly looking five or six years into the future. In fact, in most cases, your home value is still likely above your purchase price. In the end, it is important to understand that the pleasures we derived from the bull market were overshadowed by the pain inflicted by the correction. I would like to believe that we all have learned that lesson.

Part Four

Autos

20

Mike Jackson

The relationship between real estate and auto markets has always been a strong one, and the direct effect that one of these areas can have over the other has never been more pronounced than it is now. Mike Jackson, chairman and CEO of AutoNation, understands the plight of the customer better than anyone else in the business. Mike predicted the demise of the consumer about a year before it actually happened. As the largest auto retailer in the nation, one might assume that AutoNation would be suffering in the new economy, but that's not the case. Mike's no-frills, CEO style has enabled the company to withstand a downturn, the likes of which hasn't been seen since World War II. In the fourth quarter of 2008 and the first quarter of 2009, AutoNation blew by consensus and

(*continued*)

(*continued*)
made his shareholders a strong profit, which reflected in their stock rebound. Mike shares his insights on how he has maneuvered around the industry's economic potholes.

A business disaster strategy is a lot like flood insurance: You can try and do without it, but when the water starts topping the levee, you sure wish you had it.

When I joined AutoNation as chairman and CEO back in 1999, one of the first things we did was develop a worst-case scenario—for that very reason. We believed that the automotive industry remained a cyclical business with the potential for extreme peaks and valleys. Managing the peaks would be easy; the extreme valley, though, is something else. In an industry that was about to average almost 17 million units for the next seven years, we wondered how to stay profitable and manage through a collapse to 10 million units. Most of my colleagues thought I was crazy to even talk about it.

The extreme of 10 million would be a major shakeout with clear losers and winners. If you survived, you would be in a remarkable position on the other side. In our judgment, a rational, disciplined, conservative strategy would be rewarded and irrational behavior would be wiped away. So we looked hard at our company in 1999 and identified the following vulnerabilities:

1. An unfocused conglomerate
2. Overdependence on domestics for 65 percent of profits
3. Overdependence on direct lending to customers
4. Decentralized command and control
5. High fixed costs; little variability in other costs
6. Over-leveraged balance sheet

So we actually began to implement our disaster plan in 2000—eight years before the actual crisis—by taking the following steps:

1. Narrowed focus, getting out of rental cars (Alamo/National), waste business, megastores, and others.
2. Diversified away from domestics into import and premium luxury.
3. Moved from direct lending to an origination fee model.
4. Implemented common processes and technology (the operational practices—how we deal with customers, inventory, finance and insurance, vehicle sales and service—and the technological platform in back office systems we use in both dealerships and corporate offices). Reduced fixed costs; established quick variability on costs.
5. Built strong investment grade balance sheet.

The moral is this: Without acting on a strategic disaster plan years in advance, tactical responses when the storm hit would not have been enough.

Harbinger of Things to Come

Business was booming into 2005 . . . and then the housing market started cracking. This was because of autumn, and those of us whose businesses make us particularly sensitive to changes in the credit market took careful note. In fact, during an appearance on *Squawk Box,* I mentioned how the situation—particularly in California—could be a harbinger of much worse to come.

I was more right than I realized. In 2006, California's auto retailing environment started to show signs of distress, and I could tell that it was just a matter of time before the housing crisis spread, dragging auto vehicle sales along with it. By the end of the year, Florida was sinking, too, a difficult circumstance for the broader economy, of course, but also an especially troubling sign for our company. We may have the largest network of dealerships in the United States, but they're most highly concentrated in the Sunbelt, and that's where some of the biggest housing losses were occurring.

By the time we announced our fourth quarter results in January 2007, I noted during our conference call with analysts that Arizona and Nevada were the next in line. We forecast that our retail sales were headed for double-digit declines, which meant implementing our tactical disaster plan in addition to our strategic plan. That meant cutting additional costs by $100 million annually, narrowing our focus, and starting to pay down debt.

New Economy Rears Its Challenging Head

As we entered 2008, it was clear that the floodwaters were rising. There was the legitimate possibility that automotive sales could be driven down to half of what they were just a couple of years before, which would be a decline of unprecedented proportions. What had begun as a housing collapse had turned into something much worse. Every dealership group that carried large inventories was suddenly faced with hundreds and hundreds of unsalable cars, vehicles that cost them money every month they went without buyers. What was even more amazing to us was that many of these groups kept on buying *more* cars, in large part because manufacturers kept making them and putting them in the pipeline.

The summer of 2008 was a struggle. In some areas around the United States, gasoline spiked to $4.00 a gallon, which triggered the sharpest shift in consumer preference in the shortest amount of time ever. Changing over inventory was a nightmare.

Then the Lehman Brothers' bankruptcy hit. From one day to the next, a credit squeeze turned into a full-scale credit panic. Loans for our customers practically disappeared from one day to the next, for every brand, in every market; sales crashed an incremental 25 percent.

We decided immediately on September 16, 2008, that this was the big one, and all initiatives underway must double their targets in size and cut in half the timeline. This is one of those moments of truth. Is the steering wheel on the bridge truly connected?

Figure 20.1 Monthly SAAR

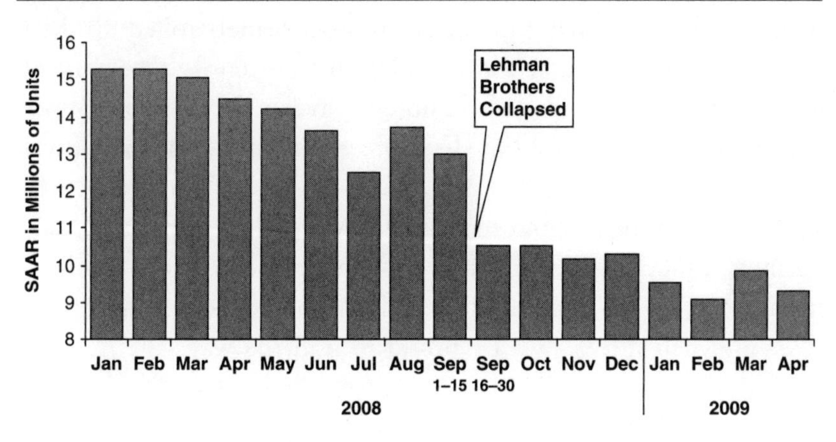

Source: Ward's and AutoNation data

Disaster Plan Put to the Test

Now the payoff of years of tedious work on processes and technology and transparency, combined with culture development, began. The next thing to figure out was how to take out cost on a fast-track basis on top of years of optimization without hurting the company's muscle. Fortunately for us, the investment we made in data systems really paid off. Ours is an industry that's still finding its way with technology, but the massive scale on which we operate requires us to invest heavily on cutting-edge technology. This turned out to give us a significant competitive advantage.

Our data mining capabilities provide immediate insights that other dealer groups can't see. They help us analyze trends at their earliest stages, and they allow us to create very accurate projections for consumer behavior. And what we saw was that the new bottom for the industry was going to be right where we predicted it.

There would be no world-ending crash, no apocalyptic meltdown. Moreover, we had accurately gauged the depth of the downturn and calibrated our business to accommodate it. Of course, none of us were happy that we had to take such drastic measures. But it was a validation that our processes did what they were supposed to: Our disaster plan accurately anticipated a long string of financial catastrophes, our top performers rolled up their sleeves and performed at a level and with an intensity that none of us had seen before, and our technology gave us the information we needed to take an appropriate level of aggressive action when it was genuinely needed.

We are optimistic about the future. During this period, irrational business models were crushed and those focused on viability, sustainability, and profitability made it to the other side of the abyss and will thrive. We are proud to lead the way.

21

Jim Lentz

When Toyota took the checkered flag in quarterly global auto sales away from General Motors in April 2007, it signaled the start of a new chapter for the auto industry. Now experts are anticipating that the Japanese automaker will knock GM out of the number one spot in the United States as early as 2010. I therefore thought it would be interesting to sit down and speak with the President of Toyota Motor Sales U.S.A. Jim Lentz to get his outlook on the challenges facing the auto industry and what the automaker is doing to thrive in this new economy.

When it comes to the nuts and bolts of the business, Lentz has seen it all. He started his career at Toyota as the

(*continued*)

(continued)
merchandising manager for its Portland region back in 1982, and he worked his way up, serving in various executive positions, including distribution manager and truck sales team member. Jim is personable and a straight shooter. He looks back at how Toyota mobilized as two enormous problems hit the industry way before the Lehman Brothers hurricane made landfall.

The auto industry was put in a very difficult position well before the collapse of Lehman Brothers and the credit crisis hit. A series of different factors unfolded, and it really was the perfect storm. The combination of the subprime housing crash with record high fuel prices, rapidly followed by a 10-year low in fuel prices, totally changed the mix of what we had to sell. You had a spike in commodity prices, and if you recall, everyone was afraid of inflation, not deflation. Lehman Brothers declared bankruptcy, and the credit crisis strikes. The stock market collapses, and for the most part, it just totally shatters consumer confidence. All of that took place in about six months. Any one of those events alone could have had a fairly significant negative impact on the industry; together, they were disastrous.

Disaster Plan

It's evident in analyzing our industry's scenario plans and business cycles from each decade that, on average, the industry dropped from peak to valley about 23 percent—a fairly tight change. The biggest drop was 25 percent, and the smallest was 21 percent. In 2000, when the industry cycle peaked at 17.4 million, one would've projected that when we saw a downturn in the economy we would have seen an industry drop to about 13.4 million. In fact, in 2008, the industry ended up even lower, at about 13.2 million. This year, we're going to be down to about 10 million—more than a 40 percent decline from peak to valley. This is beyond anyone's ability to forecast and really scenario plan around. That was the big crisis.

We have made numerous changes and established priorities to adapt to this decline, and we have truly been operating on a step-by-step basis. Our first priority was to look at restoring profitability to our operations and getting our production aligned to this new industry at 10 million. It has been a combination of reducing costs and preserving cash; monitoring our supplier network to ensure that they are strong when the cycle reverses; and all the while, guaranteeing that our manufacturing associates remain trained so that they can produce even better-quality, more efficient vehicles when we return to full production.

The second area on which we've really concentrated is maintaining the strength of our dealer network. We have worked very, *very* hard to reduce dealer inventory to get it in line with today's sales environment. The industry average for days' supply of inventory is 90 days. Our target, on the other hand, is 45 days; and we are on target. Our dealers are still profitable and investing in their facilities, their people, and their processes. So those two pieces of the puzzle are well intact. We continue to invest in products for the future, like the all-new Venza, the third-generation Prius and Lexus RX, and the all-new Lexus dedicated hybrid, the HS.

The last thing that we have done is communicate, communicate, communicate; whether it is with the parent company back in Japan, the manufacturing side, or our dealers and associates, we make sure that *everyone* understands what is happening. We will all get through this together, but the most important thing to us right now is to always continue to focus on our customer. Listening to and understanding our customer's needs and desires will allow us to build the right products and be able to weather the storm better than anybody else.

Future of Autos

You have to start by looking at macro trends, for which I'll give you a couple of examples. We look at the midterm between, say, 2010 and 2015. We understand that there will be five generations purchasing vehicles for the first time in our history when you look at our country's demographics. So whether it's more traditional buyers who are going to be purchasing and driving cars into their 90s, boomers moving into the empty nest stage, or generations X, Y, and Z, each has a very unique desire for product. Some are going to want to continue to drive traditional large vehicles. As an example, I look at myself and my parents. Basically, we bought cars by the pound. The bigger the car, the more we were willing to spend. Generation X, or especially generations Y and Z—my children—are very different. They're more likely going to purchase premium small cars. They're still going to want leather, along with the power and technology that we may expect in a more expensive car. If you go into the future beyond 2015, we continue to monitor trends that we think society is going to need for transportation.

Energy efficiency and global warming are going to drive a lot of the decisions. For example, the re-urbanization of the American cities is an important factor. According to the United Nations, in 2007—for the first time since they have been tracking—more people are living in urban centers than rural areas in the world. Cities across the country are seeing huge expansion in the urban environment. Whether it is boomers retiring or younger generations beginning to live on their own, people want to get back to the vibrancy of city life. They may want to be closer to entertainment and sports centers, reduce their commute time, or perhaps save energy; whatever the reasons, this shift back into the cities is going to impact the type and size of vehicles people buy and the fuels they'll use to power them. It may also affect how people are going to own their vehicles. We are really going to have to study ride-sharing as opposed to personal ownership. Most people today consider only two situations in terms of "getting places": public transportation or personal automobile ownership. However, the concept of ride-sharing in these urban environments is going to become much better and bigger in the future.

Urbanization also drives the need to improve engine efficiency, so the type of engines we have in cars are going to change as well. In our case, Hybrid Synergy Drive is going to remain our overall core technology, but we are also committed to developing advanced technologies. We continue to invest—even though it is a difficult time in research and development—to accelerate advancements, whether it is conventional engines or advanced technologies, plug-in hybrids, battery electrics, compressed natural gas, clean diesels, and eventually, fuel cells. It is important for us to understand all these needs, because there is no one-size-fits-all. The solution for a full-sized truck might be a clean diesel, whereas a smaller or urban vehicle may need battery electric. So we really have to push all these technologies simultaneously in an attempt to understand what transportation needs society and the consumer will have in the future. We have to see ourselves as a provider of transportation for the future, not just a manufacturer of cars and trucks.

Game Plan Timeline

We know that our current model lineup is fairly firm through 2012. We are working on preliminary plans to 2015 and on long-term plans through 2020, when it is going to take big changes in either vehicle platforms or power trains to achieve federal fuel economy and emissions standards. So you can look at short- and medium- and long-term plans, but the driver for plans beyond 10 years is energy availability—oil as we know it. One could argue that we're going to hit the oil peak within a few years, but it will likely be sometime toward the end of the next decade. I do believe that the demand for oil will far exceed its supply sometime around 2018 or 2020. The price of gasoline for cars will become so expensive that it will probably not be realistic, so we have about 10 years to figure out what the next fuel source will be. Compressed natural gas, as an example, will not reach its peak until probably 2040. So there is a time period during which compressed natural gas could play a significant role. This is why we believe so strongly in our Hybrid Synergy Drive, which basically makes an engine with electric motors capable of being fueled by a number of different types of engines. Today, it is internal combustion gas; in the future, it could be compressed natural gas or diesel, and eventually hydrogen fuel cells if needed.

What consumers today want is a stable price of fuel; and if that is $3.00 a gallon, so be it. If it is $4.00 per gallon, so be it. What consumers have a difficult time adjusting to is wide fluctuation, when one month it is $5.00, and six weeks later it's $1.75. Given that situation, it is difficult for consumers to decide on what they're going to drive. Stability is necessary, and whether stability is created by some type of gas tax or another option, our policy makers need to resolve this situation.

Weathering the Storm

We do not base our car production lineup on the price of gasoline; this is why we have been able to weather the storm better than most. We are a full-line manufacturer, and have always been. So when gas prices go up, we do not move all of our resources toward small cars. When gas prices go down, we do not move all of our resources toward full-size vehicles. It is important to offer a broad variety of products to meet individual customer needs. A customer who has a 47-mile commute will want a fuel-efficient vehicle, like a Prius; but another—say, a contractor—will want something larger, like a Tundra. So we as a brand can offer what meets the needs of both of these customers.

Circumventing the Credit Crunch

We have a captive finance company that has had adequate capital and the right amount of cash to make loans to consumers. We've seen a tightening of credit standards over time. If you look back three or four years, it was easy to buy a car with no money down. If you had a trade-in and you happened to owe more than your car was worth, it was fairly simply to finance all of that into the new purchase and just have a bigger payment. But today, as a result of the credit crisis, it is much, *much* more difficult to do.

Planning Ahead

I cannot control what is going to happen to the economy; no one can. I can only scenario plan and prepare for differing economic conditions. I can tell you that in the long run, this industry will recover. American consumers still love cars and trucks, and they love the freedom that owning cars and trucks represent. The U.S. population is still growing. Members of generation Y are just reaching their earning years, where they are going to be buying their first—or, in some cases, their second—car. Generation Z is just getting their driver's licenses, so we are looking at 2.5 million new drivers hitting the marketplace each and every year for the foreseeable future.

The economy and auto industry show recovery rates from past business cycles that bring us to annual industry sales of 16 million plus vehicles sometime in the next five or six years. The rate at which we will recover will be based on a number of things—population, number of vehicles in the household—that won't have a significant effect over the short term. Pent-up demand will also have a positive impact. There are about 250 million vehicles in operation in today's market. Typically, in an average 15-million-vehicles sales year, we are also scrapping a similar number. In 2009, we will probably scrap about 14 million vehicles, in a year when we will probably sell only about 10 million. That would be the first time that has happened since World War II. So there are going to be more people and households, but fewer vehicles; and the median age of passenger cars is at an all-time high at 9.4 years. All of these trends lead us back to the fact that there is pent-up demand, which predicts better years to come in the industry. But I do have one caveat with all that—and that is what might happen with regulation.

Caveat to Autos' Future

There is the potential that regulatory action is going to shape our—and everyone else in the industry's—future product offerings. So the question is really going to be whether this aligns with what consumers want in the long run. We have to consider the cost of compliance with government regulation, which leads us to wonder if consumers will purchase these new technologies in significant volumes to make a difference to the environment and help reduce our dependence on foreign oil. That is going to be critical. Are we going to be able to sustain the development and production of these new technologies that are profitable for automakers over time?

The industry is suffering a little bit of a hangover from the huge incentives that started at the beginning of this decade—and it has put consumers in a very difficult position to trade in cars today. This has to change, because it's not a sustainable model. After 9/11, the industry started boosting incentives on vehicles to help get America moving and keep the economy on track. Although it seemed like a pretty good idea at the time, the industry created a vicious cycle. In order to fuel incentives, we had to raise prices; and to cover the price increase, more incentives were required. Thus began this cycle of higher price, higher incentive, which, in time, was not the consumer's best friend. It didn't really respect the consumer, because someone who buys a $40,000 vehicle with a $10,000 incentive doesn't really know what they're getting into or understand some of the hidden costs on the depreciation of the vehicle. Our goal is to continue to offer great products at a great value for the consumer. In our mind, good value is where the sticker price is very close to what the consumer is going to pay for the vehicle, so there are no hidden costs over time, and we can protect the resale values.

The Toyota Way

What drives our company first and foremost—whether in good times or in bad—are the principles of "The Toyota Way," which dictate that we continue to have respect for customers. We challenge ourselves and our dealers to provide the best products and our dealers to offer the best service to customers; most importantly, we just keep moving forward. We have this concept of *kaizen,* or continuous improvement, which allows us to remain focused on satisfying our consumers' needs. So in response to the recent downturn, we have taken significant companywide cost-cutting measures. We have curbed overtime and bonuses, reduced compensation, and curtailed travel. We have considerably reduced marketing costs, and cut out a lot of the motivational programs for dealers. We've even cut out large-scale dealer meetings.

Although we've managed to save some money over the short term, the reality is that you can't save yourself into profitability. Merely cutting costs is not enough. The most vital aspect for us is to understand what gets our customers excited about products and what it takes to get them back into the showroom. In our case, that is all about product cadence and new products. Rather than cutting back, we are continuing to develop new and improved products; and our showrooms are a reflection of that. The Venza, the third-generation Prius and the new generation of the Lexus RX, or a new vehicle for Lexus called the HS (which is the first dedicated luxury hybrid) are examples of our dedication to thriving in the new economy. You realize that constantly bringing out new and fresh and exciting product will help us weather any storm.

In reality, we are an extremely resilient company. If we retain our focus on constant improvement, we are going to be pretty good. In the end, especially with everything that is going on in the industry right now, stockholders or bondholders or those granted government support or new regulations are not who will determine the success of this industry. Ultimately, customers will be the ones who influence success. Manufacturers who continue to listen to customers—those who provide quality products that are durable, dependable, and reliable; products that add value; and products that are sold and serviced through profitable and trustworthy dealers who provide an excellent experience—will be the winners.

22

Gerald Greenwald

When it comes to all things transportation, Jerry Greenwald is the expert to know. He has more than four decades of experience in the transportation sector and was chairman and CEO of UAL Corporation, parent of United Airlines, for five years. He was hired by auto legend Lee Iacocca to help lead Chrysler back from the brink in the 1980s. From 1979 through 1990, Greenwald held various executive positions with Chrysler. He served as vice chairman of the Board from 1989 to May 1990 and as chairman of Chrysler Motors from 1985 to 1988. He also held top executive positions at Ford, Dillon Read, and Olympia & York. Today, Jerry is a founder of Greenbriar Equity Group,

(*continued*)

(*continued*)
which specializes in investing in the transportation sector. He is also a member of the board of directors for Aetna.

I met Jerry through another one of my contacts, Jerry York, who was actually Greenwald's protégé back in the days of Chrysler. Since my introduction to him, I have been calling on Greenwald for his insight into the market meltdown as well as the auto crisis. His honesty and candidness are truly what lend to his credibility.

Before the meltdown, I remember saying, "You know, this is not feeling good. We better start developing some contingency plans." I went that far, but I did not go running and jumping.

Credits started to tighten up. The markets began to drag. A variety of economic indicators began to show a slowdown. Our clients are investors, who, although quite concerned, knew that we had been careful and prudent and that we would be okay no matter what was going to transpire after September 2008.

We went into motion, and our first effort was to assume for the worst and hope for the best. That meant looking at every one of our portfolio companies and going through the what-ifs and economic modeling. In almost every case, we believed that it was prudent in some combination to be sure that our credit lines were sound and our operating costs were tight.

Opportunities

There's an expression: If you're duck hunting, you don't aim the shotgun at the duck as it's flying; you aim in front of the duck. Likewise, our economic conditions are constantly in motion. We've been trying to judge the right time to get more aggressive and go into a buying mode. We look at our own industries and we listen to economists, but we don't do everything they say, because they recommend different things. We compare notes with other investors, and we're pretty close now. Will we be able to buy at bottom? I don't think so; we're not *that* good. But considering that we are going to be buying and holding for three to seven years, we don't have to buy at rock bottom, because we're not selling next week anyway.

In the meantime, we've been looking at a number of opportunities that are, in one form or another, peculiar. What do I mean by that? Well, our biggest impediment to buying is credit availability. There is little credit out there, so we look at some opportunities and think, "Well, we don't need a lot of credit to buy." A particular opportunity may be good enough that we will put in mostly equity and a little bit of debt and wait for the markets to improve. Then we'll do what we call recapitalizing, or borrowing more money and taking some of the equity out. Additionally, some really sound companies are looking for straight equity so that they can renegotiate their credit lines. There is a lot of Chinese and Middle Eastern money in the system, so we're considering some opportunities in that vein.

Creating a Strategy

We aren't very different in this setting from the day we started in business 10 years ago, although perhaps we're a bit more cautious. What do I mean? We started with a strategy that we are more than money. So many private equity firms and hedge funds take great pride in "financial engineering" and going anywhere money can be made. The founding partners were somewhat uneasy with this theme. I'm not saying it doesn't work, but we were uncomfortable being opportunists and going where every opportunity would be. We felt that we would do better if we stayed with what we know best, which is transportation.

From the day we started seeking investors, we have wanted to prove the thesis that we are more than money. We have operational experience and knowledge about all transportation sectors. We wanted to have a great mix of investment bankers, operations people, consultants, and people who grew up in the field of private equity. And we have essentially stuck to that theme.

The second belief we've stood by over the years is that it would be wrong to be overly concerned about "putting our money to work." Private equity firms typically function by creating a fund of investors, closing the fund, and then taking about six years, sometimes a little longer, to invest that money. Our approach is to be highly selective in investing that money. We would rather pick our times carefully, be patient, find the right opportunities, and then make our moves. In our 10 years, there have been occasions when we would not buy a company for a full year. We would instead use the year to keep looking and expanding our network; we wouldn't sweat our year without activity.

Buying Criteria

It is hard to describe a single most important criterion in terms of buying. We look for companies that we believe represent secular growth. In other words, they have a particular niche or particular industry with a great opportunity for ongoing growth for the next 10 years. We also look for companies with impressive brands. Having said that, we have plenty of experience among us in areas like crisis management and turnarounds. Therefore, we are not shy about identifying turnarounds that we think could add value. But for the most part, we are looking for growth and first-rate management teams with whom we want to partner.

Here are two examples from our current portfolio. About a year ago, we bought a privately held company called AmSafe that manufactures seat belts for aircraft, commercial aircraft, general aviation, and military. They have a dominant market share and an extremely smart, engineering-oriented management team. When we bought them, they had just recently received certification from the Federal Aviation Administration (FAA) for an air bag in the seat belt. We believed that the air bag seat belts have a terrific growth potential over the next several years. It is not an invention that *might* happen; we've been at it now for a year or a year and a half, and there's something like 30,000 seats in the air with these air bags in the seat belts. The next time you are on an airplane, turn your seatbelt buckle upside down, and you'll probably see AmSafe as the brand on that buckle.

The other is a company called EMD, Electro-Motive Diesel. We bought this locomotive manufacturing business from General Motors, and we saw this company as a great brand. There are only two companies in the world that manufacture these heavy-duty locomotives. GM was concentrating on cars and trucks and wanted to sell EMD.

We saw this as a fantastic opportunity to work with a great brand, a well-engineered product, and a company that we thought we could turn around and develop; there was also a potential for secular growth in the market. It's been four years, and the company has been turned from losses to profits and has gone from having sales of about $800 million to just under $2 billion in revenue (excluding this downturn). EMD has expanded from a North American to a worldwide business. We have been stressing to our new management team at EMD that the customer really matters. They have turned around the company's reputation. We are very pleased with how EMD is developing.

Future of the Transportation Industry

Our transportation sector is comprehensive—air, ground, and sea principal companies, services, and suppliers. The airline industry is a growth industry, but the problem for years—and it's hardly a joke—has been that it is one of the few growth industries that has figured out how to *lose* money. So we have tried to pick the places where members of the industry make profits. For example, one of the first companies in which we invested is called Hexcel. It's a public company that started about 50 years ago making skis out of composites. Today, they manufacture a wide array of very light-weight products for commercial and military aircraft. Although we don't normally invest in public companies, we felt very strongly after 9/11 that this growth industry was going to experience an upturn in manufacturing of aircraft for commercial use after the ensuing recession among Boeing, Airbus, and others. And once that happened, Hexcel (a supplier of parts) was going to see a corresponding upturn with the industry again.

Another appealing feature of this company was that it was one of only two or three suppliers who have learned to produce very lightweight components for aircraft—composites, not aluminum or other metals. We believe that as new platforms, such as the A380 Airbus or 787 Boeing are introduced into the market, they would shift away from aluminum to these kinds of parts. Finally, we loved the management team at Hexcel. They were dedicated, but they got caught in the enormous downturn in the industry, and their banks were leaning on them. We thought we could make an equity investment and use that investment as incentive for the Hexcel banks to renegotiate their terms and conditions. We also thought that we could be of some help to the management. Because of our network, we knew the senior people who were their customers. But for the most part, we were just good board members. Three years later, we sold our shares.

We join the boards for companies when we invest. In the case of Hexcel, the management and other members of the board liked one of our guys (my partner Joel Beckman) so much that even *after* we sold all our shares, they asked him to stay on as a board member, which he has done.

Airline Turbulence

North American Airlines has struggled the most within the airline industry, and the main reason for this is that the unions have not been able to think long-term for their members. This means that too often, these groups—particularly the pilots' unions—have been quick to scoop up profits. The moment it looked like an airline was starting to make a profit, the unions would take the money off the table for their members and threaten to shut the place down if refused.

One answer to this situation might be a baseball-type arbitration, which would require congressional approval. It sounds kind of off-the-wall, I know, but it might provide the right motivation if the two parties could not reach an agreement. The arbitrator would decide on the next contract. Each side could submit a contract, but the arbitrator could not average. He would have to pick one or the other. As a result, both parties would submit more responsible proposals.

Auto Transformation

To start with, I thank my lucky stars for not having done proper due diligence when Lee Iacocca asked me to come to Chrysler back in 1979; if I had, I would have been scared to death and not gone there. But I signed on and it was the experience of my life. There I was, essentially doing fine as a pitcher in the minor leagues, and some guy came in and said, "Hey, you want to pitch in the World Series?" That's how it all started for me.

But when I had been there for just four or five weeks (Iacocca had arrived just months before), I realized it was a mess. It was just awful. The very first thing we stopped doing was building cars on speculation. Most car companies get orders from dealers, and the cars get built. The moment the cars are ready, the dealers pay for them at regular standard prices. If a car company builds cars on speculation, it is fudging the books. Financials may temporarily look good, but it is a killer, because the dealers soon catch on, and they say, "No, I don't want to buy the cars you have already built. I want to buy the cars that you *haven't* built yet." And pretty soon the factory is forced to give discounts to dealers to take the cars that were built on speculation, and their quality isn't as good. They have been sitting in parking lots all over the Midwest. Once started, this cycle is not so easy to stop. We had cars in parking lots all over the place, and it took us a year to finally sell the last of them. The last were specialty trucks and they were sold for $0.35 on the dollar. But we cleaned it up, and we stopped.

The people in the company had no clue about their warranty costs and the primary reasons for them. Warranty costs essentially help a car company learn where the quality defects are by looking through warranty claims. You can then set assignments among engineers and manufacturing people, find the top 10 defects, and decide who is going to be accountable for getting them fixed. That was one of the early things we started.

This may sound too technical, but at that time, Chrysler did not understand car options—or what percent of them were being ordered for a particular automobile type. Options are more profitable than the cars themselves. If you can figure option rates and which are most profitable, you can find ways to dramatically increase profitability per car by helping to manage them. But if you don't have any way of knowing the quantity of options being bought and what the profits are on them, you are blind. It took a few months, but we put in systems and managed options.

Déjà Vu

In the end, we needed to build cars people wanted and that we could make money selling. When we arrived, the cars were gas-guzzlers and not of very good quality. This is déjà vu, right? But then we had a car that changed all that: the K-car. It was started by Hal Sperlich, who had left Ford before Iacocca and I came to Chrysler. The K-car was to be the most fuel-efficient six-passenger car in the world, with a four-cylinder engine. That got us started; and we went back to Washington and we made claims that we would be able to find our way home financially because of this car.

After that, some of the same guys with Iacocca—as well as Iacocca himself—created the minivan. We did research on it, and the consumer said, "Why would you want to build that? Where's the trunk? Where's the hood? It looks like a breadbasket!" And yet we were convinced that once we actually started selling them, people would want them. And we took our chances.

Those were kind of crazy days, but I remember it still as if it were today. Hal Sperlich, the guy who had been working on the minivan, and I were in the design center, and one of my finance guys came in with the news that it would cost us $700 million for tooling the minivan. And although $700 million might not sound like much today, it was for us back then. I can recall telling him that we simply didn't have that kind of money. But then Hal and I looked at each other and said, "Well, we don't have *any* money, so what's another $700 million? Let's get started, and we'll figure out how to come up with the money." After the minivan, our next car was the Jeep Cherokee, which came after we bought American Motors.

So what is my message here? The product, the product, the product! You cannot save your way out of a crisis. You cannot cut your costs enough to become successful. If you are a service company, you have got to have really good service—it's that simple. If you are a product company, you have to have superb product, or nothing is going to save you. So we bet all our horses on new product, but it was pretty obvious we were running out of cash.

I was sent to Washington, DC, to plead our case. One of the things I learned in Washington was from an old political warrior, Tip O'Neill, who said, "Listen, sonny; in Washington, you can be dead right, but you can still be dead." We were pitching an argument that the government—who was imposing all these fuel economy increases and emissions reductions—should give us a tax credit because as the smallest of the "big three," we were paying more money per car than our competitors. Fixed costs were spread over fewer cars. After about 30 days, Washington was starting to laugh at us, but the argument was actually logical.

Finally others in the administration came up with an idea that we might be able to make a case for loan guarantees, and this is what started us on the right path. I learned a lot about Washington. I literally had an office in the basement of the Treasury department, because we were so intertwined and influenced by what was going on down there. After all was said and done, we had a better product and costs were down; we had 10 years to pay off those loans, but we needed only four.

Paying Uncle Sam Back

Chrysler and GM are going to need to do this the moment they come out of bankruptcy. We almost didn't care about anything else financially; we cared about getting to what we called "cash break even." And we weren't going to do it by stopping new product investment. We kept hammering at our costs and finding new ways to generate cash.

First, we changed the payment terms for dealers. They had to take cars literally the *moment* they went over a yellow line in each assembly plant; and if they needed to borrow money, they could borrow it from our finance company. We extended payment terms with our suppliers to 45 days, which for the most part, still exist 30 years later in the industry. If you run the math on that, you create cash really fast when car sales start going up. In fact, I always wanted to say to my guys, "It's not our cash permanently, because if sales ever turn down, all that money is going to pour back out." But our sales kept creeping up, and that helped a lot to create the cash we needed to pay back Uncle Sam.

Fast-Forward to Today

What has happened to the Big Three has been quite a shock to me. I did not think that I had any emotional ties to the auto industry anymore. After all, the last time I worked at an auto company was in

1990, and that was 19 years ago. I couldn't help from reminiscing when I worked for Ford at a time when the car companies were the king. I got sent out to build companies in other countries, and in the process, I would teach others how to make cars. Now, the Big Three are at the bottom of the hill trying to survive, which is upsetting.

Optimistically, Ford will stay on its feet on its own. It will continue to prosper or will start doing so when the economy comes back. GM has downsized and has come out of bankruptcy with a much better competitive cost structure and the opportunity to start growing again. Chrysler has also emerged from bankruptcy and now with a partnership with Fiat has a new lease on life as Chrysler Group.

In any case, the auto industry, which I believe is about the toughest industry in the world in which to succeed, is going to get even tougher.

Steps for Autos to Thrive

Years ago, when I was in the auto business, there would be moments when we were having a drink or we would be between meetings and someone would say, "Wow, this is the toughest industry in the world." And I would think, "Gee, isn't that self-serving." Now I've been in five industries, and I can still claim that auto is the toughest industry in the world. It's so difficult because you have to be brave enough to start on a billion-dollar project for one new car platform three years in advance of selling it—and be smart enough to figure out how it can succeed. In addition, if it is a fair-sized car company, you have 10 of these projects going on at any one time. You are also trying to figure out what your competition is going to be doing, so it's tricky. Then, in order to succeed, you need to manufacture in several countries and deal with the political, industrial, and union issues in all of them, as well as the dealer organizations and an enormous world-wide supply base.

The Nuts and Bolts of the Auto Industry

Ask yourself how many parts there are in a car. If you count an engine as one, the answer would be 4,000 parts. But if you say, "Well, wait a minute, the engine has *x* number of parts . . ." there are 40,000 parts that go into one car. And every one of those parts has to show up at a plant on time every day, and be on time and of good quality.

There is always excess production capacity around the world. You hear people say that one of the problems of the auto industry is that there is too much capacity; if GM and Chrysler downsize, that would be good. But that is not going to solve the problem of extra capacity. The Chinese and Indians are adding more capacity, and we haven't heard from the Russians yet. So it's an industry with excess capacity all the time.

Green Push

I am oversimplifying a little bit, but the only push in North America for small cars that are high-tech and highly fuel efficient is coming from Washington and a few environmentalists. That's it. Why? Because the price of gasoline is down. The notion that Americans are going to rush to small, fuel-efficient cars out of a sense of contributing to reduce global warming is something I really doubt. We've seen it before. When the price of gasoline was $4.00, nobody wanted to buy pickups and SUVs; everybody was rushing to buy cars like the Prius. Right now, with gasoline costs around $2.00 to $3.00, small cars are not hot. And not just because the economy is soft. There used to be 16 million cars being purchased per year; that number is now around 10 million. The number one selling car is a V-8 pickup again, not a sedan.

There is also an underlying safety issue that we haven't talked about. Many people believe that SUVs are safer than smaller cars, because if you consider the statistics, you see that drivers of small cars get hurt more often than drivers of large cars. But the issue is really physics. If a 2,000-pound object collides with a 4,000-pound object, the 4,000 pound object always wins. SUVs are 4,000 or 5,000 pounds, whereas smaller cars are 2,000 or 2,500 pounds. If all cars on the roads are lightweight, they will be safe; and at $4.00 per gallon, people are going to want small cars. *Not* true at $2.00. The price of oil is so volatile over a two- to five-year period, and car companies are trying to figure out which new cars to invest in and introduce to the market. That's part of why this industry is so tough.

Investing Strategies

If you are a long-term investor, on the macro level, you need to believe the economy is going to get better. However, it seems to me it would be naïve to assume that it is ever going to get as frothy as it was two years ago, when an investor could get all the credit he or she needed to buy a company, an office building, a hotel, leverage to trade equities, or a house. *That* is not coming back—at least not anytime soon. But our economy is going to strengthen again, and people like me are trying to figure out when we hit bottom and have confidence that if we get close to a bottom and buy, we will be fine. Then there are those who say, historically, certain sectors come back early and some of them come back late. You can kind of count on that sequencing as you invest.

Thriving Indicators

I've always preached that the person responsible for others in the workplace needs to remind himself or herself that we spend most of our waking hours working, and there's got to be some element of fun and enthusiasm in it or the boss isn't doing his job. So here we are in a nasty recession and unemployment is ugly, but there needs to be some measure of enjoyment and excitement in investing.

Something Iacocca once said to me about building a management team—advice that I've been using to this day—is the following: If you are the leader, it is so much easier to slow down 10 stallions you have than it is to get 10 mules to keep going.

Since we invest in the whole sector of transportation, we have windows into a lot of the indicators. When will our railroads again start to order capital goods? That is one of the indicators. When will truck fleets start to buy new equipment again? The quantities of goods and passenger movement are strong indicators. We watch all these, and that helps give us confidence when it's time to come back in.

Part Five

Retail

23

Steve Sadove

It's hard enough dealing with an ailing economy in the here and now, but imagine trying to anticipate the confidence and buying trends of consumers at least six months in advance. That's what Saks CEO Steve Sadove has to do. The September free fall hurt everyone, especially retailers. (See Figure 23.1.)

Total retail sales were down 10.6 percent in December, and inventories were brimming after the consumer fell off a cliff. The statistics were even worse in the luxury sector. Steve

(continued)

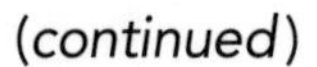

(continued)

Figure 23.1 Total Retail Sales (Year-over-Year Percent Change)

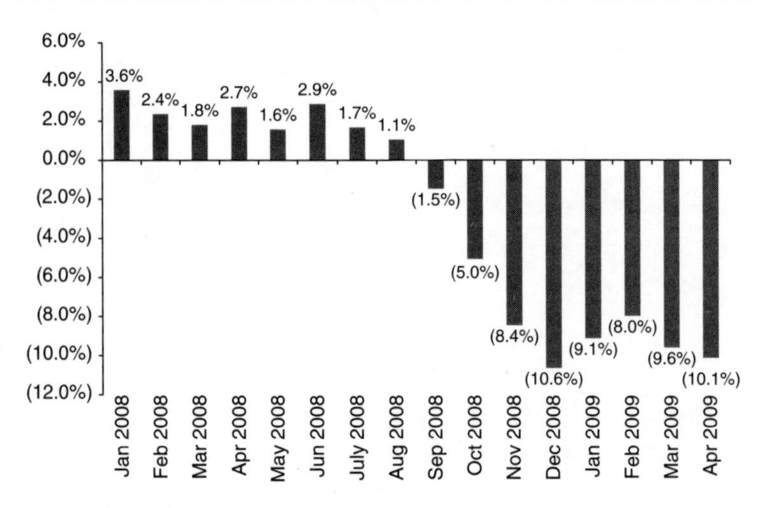

Source: Telsey Advisory Group

has been able to cut costs and strike a delicate balance between demand and inventory. Along the way, he's created a new corporate culture that he says will be Saks' new norm.

In 2007, Saks' comparable store sales grew by double digits. Even in the fourth quarter of 2007, revenues increased by approximately 10 percent. In the luxury retail business, we must try to accurately anticipate customer demand six to nine months in advance, as that is when orders are placed for merchandise. As we began to plan our fall 2008 business in late 2007, we believed we were being conservative, assuming that luxury sales would slow down somewhat but that we would still achieve some modest year-over-year growth. By early 2008, we had begun to experience some retrenching of "aspirational" customers (that is, customers for whom our items are infrequent, luxury purchases), but our core, higher-end customer was still holding up pretty well. We started to see a gradual slowdown in overall sales throughout the early part of 2008. Our comparable store sales grew in the 4 to 5 percent range in the first quarter, and we were flat in the second quarter. However, the higher-end customer within our portfolio was still experiencing a double-digit growth rate through the middle of the year.

Volatility and Consumer Confidence

In mid-2008, as the stock market became increasingly unstable and started experiencing significant drops, we began to see more volatility in our business. With the September 2008 Lehman Brothers' bankruptcy, the stock market began what felt like a free fall, and our core consumers started freezing in terms of their behavior. It was a shock to the system. The consumers at the high end, who had been the most stable and were holding up the best, suddenly turned into the ones that were performing most poorly. Sales in the luxury sector are closely correlated with the financial markets. (See Figure 23.2.)

Customers became increasingly reluctant to shop as they watched their net worths plummet by 40 percent or more. Our double-digit growth quickly reversed to double-digit sales declines. The luxury retailer was in some ways next to the financial markets, probably in the eye of the storm.

The shopping spree that many people had been on for years suddenly came to a halt. So that's the backdrop in terms of what we had to think about and how we had to manage. We were now operating in a whole new world.

Too Much Inventory

In light of the significant sales declines, we were sitting on a lot of inventory, probably several hundred million dollars too much. The "system"—meaning Saks Fifth Avenue, the luxury vendors, and the other high-end competitors—had hundreds and hundreds

Figure 23.2 Luxury Retail Sales versus Saks, Inc.

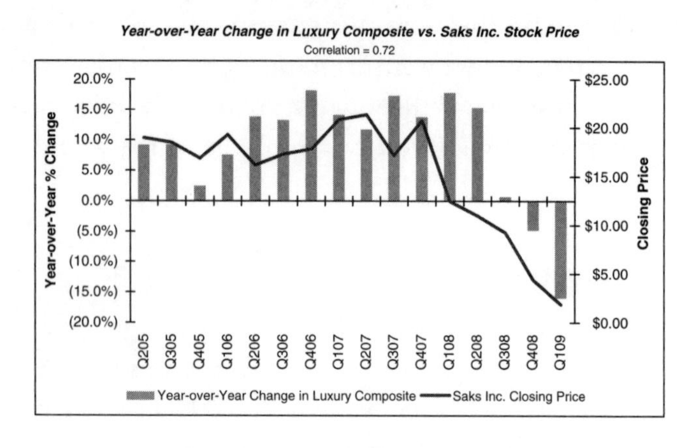

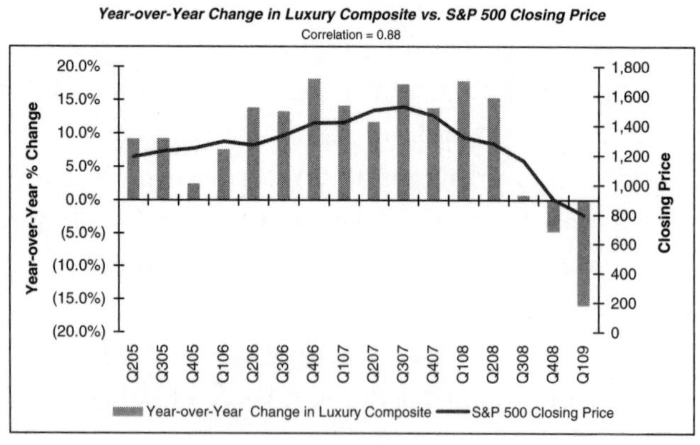

*1Q09 Year-over-year change excludes Hermes and LVMH because they have not reported.

Source: Telsey Advisory Group

of millions of dollars of too much product. So we were dealing with excess merchandise and a business and industry substantially smaller than they had been. The disconnect between supply and demand was widening.

Priority one was quickly clearing excess inventory. To do this, we had to take some rather extraordinary markdowns, and the pricing actions we took resulted in the consumer getting some great deals. We were very proactive and aggressive about getting the two in line so that when we entered 2009, the company would have a more balanced inventory position. It was difficult, because we took it on the chin relative to our gross margin rate, but we quickly cleared the products, which was the absolute right thing to do. However, it was painful from a financial perspective, and we lost a lot of money in the fourth quarter of 2008.

New Economy Strategy

With the recent downturn, we nimbly and quickly shifted the focus of our organization from operating a high-growth business to managing a smaller sales base. A cultural evolution within the organization was taking place. The past became a lot less relevant, and we started thinking differently about every aspect of our business. There are three things I would call out as being critical to manage through and to win in this new economy: controlling what you can control; listening to your customers and making needed strategic shifts to the company's business model to accommodate the changing environment and consumer desires; and communicating thoroughly, thoughtfully, and frequently.

Controlling What We Can Control

With sales trending in excess of 20 percent below prior year levels, we began keenly focusing on what we could control—our capital spending, our inventory purchases, and our expenses. We started to think about managing our business for cash and ensuring that we remained financially solid and that we emerged an even stronger business when the economic conditions improved.

Although we cut our annual capital spending by nearly 60 percent and reduced inventory purchases by 20 percent in 2009, I was especially pleased with how the organization approached and embraced right-sizing the organization and cost structure for the lower sales base. Between the third fiscal quarter of 2008 and the second fiscal quarter of 2009, we reduced selling, general, and administrative expenses by over $125 million, which certainly exceeded our expectations and those of the investment community. These reductions reflected some hard decisions, such as reducing our workforce by approximately 17 percent and cutting management salaries, and included reductions in essentially every area of the business, from travel to supplies to benefits to marketing to information technology. We left no stone unturned. We approached every area of the business asking, "How should we do it going forward?" not, "How did we do it in the past?" As a result, we identified and began implementing cost reductions beyond what we originally anticipated. The cost reductions were significant; however, we were very cautious in areas where we interface with the consumer as we continue to place the utmost importance on further enhancing our service levels.

I would be very surprised if this belt-tightening doesn't become the new norm and stay with us. As they say, "Don't let a recession go to waste," and we don't intend to. As the economy improves, the lessons learned of reducing costs, spending money more wisely, and managing for cash are a part of our culture.

Pulse of the Consumer

Our goal remained constant: to win with our merchandise, service, and marketing strategies. We had to ensure that these strategies were the right ones to meet the desires of our customers and the changing environment. In the spring of 2009, we conducted research with thousands of existing and potential customers. Although feeling a lot less wealthy than in the past, the research confirmed that the luxury consumer still liked to shop, appreciated brands even more than before, had developed a heightened service expectation, and was searching for value more than ever—with value not just defined by price but by quality, workmanship, and uniqueness as well.

Although the research reinforced our belief that we were generally on track with our strategies, we took the findings and made necessary adjustments to our initiatives in order to gain market share in the new environment. We collaborated closely with our vendor partners to create merchandise that our customers would appreciate and value. Our customers love brands, and they like things that are special and exclusive—but they want a fair value in what they're buying. We worked to ensure that we offered the right balance of "good," "better," and "best" luxury merchandise in each of our stores. "Clienteling," building relationships, and providing exceptional service became more critical than ever. Every store developed a local business plan and began taking ownership of expanding their market share by identifying potential customers and how to improve relationships with them.

Communicating

Integral to reshaping the organization's culture and thinking was communicating to the associates and making sure that they understood why we were doing what we were doing—from reducing costs to adjusting our merchandising strategies. One of the most impactful things I did, beginning in October 2008, was to create "Straight Talk with Steve."

Every two weeks or so, I would spend five minutes video recording a message to all associates from my office in which I described what we were doing and why, basically sharing whatever was on my mind. (See the photo on the following page.) Then we would send it out to our 12,000 employees. It became a way to keep everybody apprised on a very frequent basis about what was happening in the organization. My direct reports were doing similar kinds of things. So I was leading the charge in communicating, getting everyone involved, and making everyone part of the process. In fact, "Straight Talk with Steve" continues today.

The remarkable thing about this unprecedented period was that the morale throughout all levels of the company held up amazingly well. I believe that because we treated people with dignity and

Figure 23.3 "Straight Talk with Steve"

respect and communicated so frequently and so thoroughly, our associates understood that we weren't alone in this—and that what we were doing was necessary for the survival of the company.

Being the CEO of a company includes being its chief cheerleader. In communicating, you have to be fact- and reality-based, but you must also express optimism and confidence that we can not only survive but win in the long term.

I am excited about the future of the country, the retail sector, and Saks. I have never seen the industry so energized about the changes that are taking place. I see better days ahead. We are not letting a recession go to waste.

Part Six

Opportunities

24

Wilbur Ross

The leaders in the new economy are the ones who are picking through the carnage to uncover opportunities at prices that may never be seen again in this generation. One investor who's known for having the panache to turn around "bad" investments is Wilbur Ross. For more than four decades, Wilbur has become the undisputable king in spotting troubled companies and turning them around. Although many people characterize him as a "vulture" investor, Wilbur really is the discerning judge of dying companies.

Wilbur's Wall Street fame began when he purchased the failing steel companies LTV and Bethlehem Steel and created International Steel Group (ISG). In 2005, he sold ISG to ArcelorMittal, the world's largest steel company, for $4.5 billion. His firm, WL Ross & Co., made $2.5 billion from that deal, and Ross himself took home a reported $300 million.

(*continued*)

(*continued*)

After that, Wilbur created International Coal Group out of the bankrupt Horizon Natural Resources in 2004 and has since set his sights on the new economy's troubled assets: failing banks like BankUnited, struggling real estate finance companies such as Assured Guaranty and American Home Mortgage Servicing, as well as the auto suppliers.

Wilbur along with Richard LeFrak has combined their real estate and financial prowess in creating the joint venture WLR LeFrak. In addition to investing in failed Florida bank BankUnited, the group was part of a consortium that announced in October of 2009 they would acquire $4.5 billion in real estate assets from failed Chicago-based bank Corus Bank Real. Valuing around $2.77 billion, the transaction at the time was one of the largest acquisitions of distressed commercial real estate assets.

For about nine years, I have worked with Wilbur on the numerous corporate announcements he has made as well as his guest co-hosting gigs on *Squawk Box*. His approach to a deal is very interesting; I enjoy hearing about how he can slice through what many investors may think is garbage. He is able to buy a company and transform it into a profitable business—and that is what makes him one of the best businessmen of his time.

At 8:30 A.M. Singapore time on Monday, September 15, 2008, I was walking across Orchard Street from an interview on CNBC's *Asia Squawk Box* to my meeting with Madam Ho, CEO of Temasek and a major investment arm of the government. My BlackBerry rang with an excited call from our portfolio manager, David Storper: "Bank of America is acquiring Merrill, and Lehman will file bankruptcy tomorrow."

I was stunned. Bank of America had been expected to acquire Lehman Brothers, and there was not even a whisper that Merrill

Lynch needed to be taken over. In fact, CEO John Thain had raised billions of dollars of equity for Merrill Lynch—some of it from Temasek. David had checked on our exposures and reported that we had a small amount of dollar-yen swap with Lehman Brothers; Lehman Brothers was on the profitable side, and therefore we had no credit risk. One of our portfolio companies, Montpelier Reinsurance, also had some minor direct holdings. That was good news, because recoveries would likely be pennies on the dollar. But what did these surprises mean? We concluded that both Lehman Brothers and Merrill Lynch must have more severely toxic assets than had been thought. That meant the same would have to be true of other financial institutions—and with the economy already teetering, that could lead to a credit crunch with serious implications for all businesses. To protect ourselves against what could be a hostile credit environment, we promptly contacted the CEOs of each of our portfolio companies with the following suggestions:

"No one knows for sure how severe the problems of our financial system are, but we interpret the events of this past weekend as portending a new credit crunch on top of the economy's existing weakness. Therefore, please assume that you will likely find it challenging to achieve your budgets from now through 2009. As a result, prudence dictates slowing or eliminating capital expenditures for growth, even tighter working capital constraints, expansion of committed bank lines wherever possible, and drawing down lines well before you actually need the cash. Since these moves will impact negatively our immediate earnings, it is appropriate to modify downward the earnings target of your bonus formula. Finally, we must be even more conservative than usual in the earnings and cash flow assumptions on which we base acquisition bids."

As the Temasek meeting began, Madam Ho broke the ice by joking that since Bear Stearns had failed on my prior visit and Lehman Brothers and Merrill Lynch this time, that I should promise not to return to Singapore soon because they did not want another crisis. The rest of the meeting went more or less normally.

Over dinner that night at the improbably named Palm Beach Crab House, my colleagues and I mainly discussed the implications again. The U.S. and Asian markets had tanked according to the news, and the talking heads were shocked. Like the rest of the investment community, and probably the broader public, our first questions were, "Who's next?" and "How much of a domino effect will there be?"

It didn't take long to find out. By the time we got to Tokyo for our major investor conference, a domino had fallen—and a major one at that. AIG was taken over by the government because its enormous exposure to derivatives—which had been problematic even before Lehman Brothers collapsed—now became totally unmanageable. For as long as one could remember, AIG had been an unimpeachable AAA credit, and although it had gone through an accounting scandal a few years earlier, there hadn't been major rumors of its insolvency. One could only wonder whether AIG might not have failed if Lehman Brothers had been saved.

To me, AIG's failure was the more frightening of the two, because AIG was a problem not just for Wall Street but also for Main Street. It was the largest U.S. insurance company and had millions of policy holders in the United States and Asia. My forthcoming speech became even more bearish than the earlier draft. As far back as January 2007, I told attendees at a Credit Suisse Asset-Backed Securities Conference that the bubble was bursting. It had seemed clear even then that the lack of inflation-adjusted median income growth from 2000 to 2006 had caused American families to over-leverage themselves, because that was the only way they could live a little better each year. Rising residential real estate prices and ever-more-generous mortgage securitizations continually inflated each other's bubbles and made this leveraging possible. Securitizations accounted for half of all the consumer credit in the United States, and many of the credit derivative swaps (CDS) were issued to hedge the credit risk of securitizations. Thus, the CDS market disruption would create yet another problem for securitizations to overcome. With less credit, the outlook for home and automobile sales would become very weak. For example, in 2007, 1 million cars were purchased by families using proceeds from remortgaging their homes. Compounding the problem would be the loss of consumer confidence as household name financial institutions went up in smoke.

For all these reasons, we decided to temporarily suspend new commitments in the WLR Recovery Fund IV, our most recent long-only fund. It was about 25 percent committed, and because it cannot sell stocks short, the only way for it to be defensive was to stay uninvested. The commitments that it had made were generally in non-public companies, so there was no realistic way to sell them.

We also decided to sharpen our focus and to put our major efforts into financial services. That was clearly the epicenter of the economic earthquake and most difficult to analyze, because it required one to make judgments about how bad and for how long the economy would get and then translate that into credit judgments about the portfolios of individual institutions. That level of complexity and risk taking would keep most investors out, especially given that the recent rounds of both private and public financings in that sector had already produced terrible results. For example, Lehman Brothers had privately raised some $5.5 billion of private equity less than six months before it folded and rendered these investments worthless. We had participated that weekend in a whirlwind round of due diligence but fortunately dropped out because we concluded that management was not sufficiently candid about their real estate holdings. As it turned out, real estate was the principal cause of their demise.

We initially settled on four sectors: mortgage servicing, monoline insurance, commercial banks, and thrifts. We already had invested in American Home Mortgage Services. It had met or exceeded budget each month, so we were comfortable about analyzing servicing and achieving high rates of return from it. The analytical keys were: (1) to estimate the so-called roll rate—at which borrowers who were paying on time would become progressively more delinquent; (2) to forecast how many of those would be foreclosed; (3) to determine how long it would take to foreclose and sell the property; and (4) to determine what percentage of the good payers would sell their homes voluntarily or refinance them. These factors would determine both how long we would retain the stream of monthly servicing fees and how much capital would be tied up making advances on behalf of delinquent borrowers. The advances were creditworthy because they rank senior to the mortgage and must be paid first, but they did consume capital at a low rate of return. It turned out that we were able to buy a lot more servicing at a high all-in rate of return. As of May 2009, eight months after Lehman Brothers fell—our company has become the largest independent servicer of non-prime mortgages at $106 billion and is earning at the rate of $130 million per year. In a different environment, it probably would have taken several years to achieve that level of earnings.

Monoline insurance was our second target. There had originally been half a dozen of these companies that had AAA ratings and provided credit enhancement to municipal bonds, securitizations, and infrastructure project financings. Most of them were being downgraded—in some cases, by several notches—because of poor risk management. The municipal part of the business had a relatively low-risk profile, but many of the securitizations, especially ones backed by mortgages, proved to be quite toxic. Most of the monolines, such as Ambac, committed a cardinal sin of risk management by owning in their portfolios similar credit risks to what they were insuring. This meant that if their default rate assumptions proved to be too low, as they did, then the monoline would be hit by the double whammy of insurance and portfolio losses. The insurance exposure alone was many times the shareholders' equity, so the specter of insolvency loomed large.

But one company seemed different: Assured Guaranty. Its CEO, Dominic Frederico, had a home a few miles from my principal residence in Palm Beach, so I asked another Palm Beacher, Bill Bartholomay, the Vice Chairman of Willis Group Holdings (an insurance brokerage group), to make the introduction. Dominic came to my home, and we hit it off personally; but more importantly, I was impressed by his command of details of both the insurance and investment portfolios, and by their concepts of risk management. The investments were, on average, AA rated and substantively different credits from the A and BAA issues they typically enhanced. After a few more meetings and field due diligence, it seemed clear that in an imploding industry, Assured Guaranty would be the last one left standing with high credit ratings. That meant it was in a position both to gain market share organically and to either reinsure or acquire existing insurance volumes from companies with capital problems. Assured Guaranty's stock was down 30 percent from its high 12 months earlier. It also seemed statistically cheap, because it was trading modestly below its book value, but at only half the sum of its book value and the present value of its future premiums (PVP).

PVP is unique to the monoline insurers. It arises from the fact that municipalities pay a single premium at the time the coverage of the life of the bond issue is underwritten, sometimes as long as 30 years. But the accounting rules require the premium to be taken into income proportionately over the life of the bond, thereby locking in many years of 100 percent predictable revenues. Assured Guaranty had generated a non–balance sheet asset of PVP roughly equal to its book value, which was growing daily; so at less than one half the sum of book value and equity, it seemed very attractive. We agreed to invest $250 million at a discount from market and committed to invest another $750 million over the next year for deals at a discount from the then-market, subject to a floor and a ceiling price, and Assured Guaranty's retention of its AAA stable ratings. This gave the company the war chest it needed for acquisitions. A few months later, we helped them negotiate the highly complex but also highly accretive acquisition of FSA from Dexia, a large European financial services company. FSA's insurance and investment portfolios had manageable problems, but like AIG, they had written vast amounts of guaranteed investment contracts and other derivatives in their financial products division that were billions of dollars under water—and getting worse every day. The trick was to pay for the insurance business in stock, a deal that would be highly accretive to Assured Guaranty, but to insulate the merged company from the toxicity of the financial products division. Ultimately, the French and Belgian governments, who had by now nationalized Dexia, provided Assured Guaranty with indemnification.

Banks and thrifts were the other targets. We already had made a joint venture with John Kanas to find a regional bank, infuse capital into it, install John as the CEO, and then roll up other depositary institutions in the same region, creating one large enough either to trade actively on the New York Stock Exchange at a decent multiple or to be acquired by one of the major domestic or foreign holding companies. John, 62, had taken charge of North Fork Bank in Mattituck, Long Island, when it had $20 million of deposits and built it up to $60 billion before selling it to Capital One at 3.5 times its book value. He had made a couple of hundred million dollars for himself out of the deal and had served out his non-compete agreement. He didn't need a job, but he needed a big pocketbook; so we agreed to back him for up to $1 billion. Combining a meaningful capital base with John's excellent reputation with bankers and regulators meant that we would get a look at essentially every troubled bank.

But there were some difficult regulatory issues that needed to be resolved. Since we believed that our targets would be billions of dollars insolvent, we would need the Federal Deposit Insurance Corporation (FDIC) to seize the institution and fill a lot of the hole. Otherwise, more private capital would be required than could be justified by future earnings. The problem was that FDIC's practice had been to confine the bidding for failed banks to other banks and to seize the failed institution on a Friday evening and reopen it as the acquiring bank on Monday at 9:00 A.M. But our fund was not a bank or a bank holding company—and did not want to become one. Doing so would have required us to divest of our non-financial assets and never acquire any in the future. To avoid this problem, we could not own more than 24.9 percent of the holding company. That problem could be solved by joining with other investors, as we soon did with Blackstone, Carlyle, Centerbridge, LeFrak Organization, and others. But, how do you become qualified as a bank or a bank holding company without being one so that you can be a bidder?

Eventually, we reached an agreement with the regulators that the management team and investors would file a holding company application that would be complete, except for the identity and deal terms of the target. The regulators then would do their background checks, etc., and be ready to approve the application concurrently with FDIC approval of our bid.

On Thursday, May 21, 2009, at 6:00 P.M., the FDIC announced that we had taken over BankUnited for an investment of $900 million immediately after the FDIC had seized it. FDIC also announced that they estimated that the cost to them would be $4.9 million. BankUnited is the largest independent depositary institution in Florida, with $12 billion of deposits and 85 branches running north along the east coast of the state from Boca Raton. It has about 2 percent of all the deposits in Florida, even though there are many important markets, like Tampa, Orlando, St. Petersburg, Palm Beach, and Jacksonville, where it is not yet represented. In addition to the potential of de novo branches, Florida has more than 60 banks, which we believe are or soon will be insolvent and therefore distressed takeover targets. They, like BankUnited, are being brought down by bad real estate investments, one of the main reasons why Lehman Brothers failed and Merrill Lynch had to be taken over in September 2008. The long-term objective would be to create a holding company that was making a sufficiently high return on capital that it would be worth two or more times a book value higher than today's because of retention of earnings. Given the quality of management, the due diligence that was performed by a 20-person team, and the loss sharing arrangement with FDIC, the downside seems very limited. Therefore, the risk-adjusted rate of return is very high.

In general, we had correctly identified the opportunities that the financial malaise would create for us; but we did underestimate the problems that would arise for the auto industry. Our principal investment in that arena was International Automotive Components (IAC), which we had begun creating in October 2005. We did so by buying parts of the notorious bankruptcy of Collins & Aikman and supplementing them with Lear Corporation's Interior Plastics Division, by buying Mitsuboshi Belting Kaseihin in Japan and by restructuring PLASCAR in Brazil. In 2007 and the early part of 2008, all of these units were operating in line with or better than budget, and we were on our way to about $5.5 billion of sales.

But the American Axle strike in the second quarter shut down some GM plants, creating a minor problem. Our real problems in both the United States and Europe started within weeks after the fateful phone conversation in Singapore. People simply stopped buying cars. In retrospect, it should have been obvious that a credit crunch would be especially bad for autos, since a car is most households' second largest purchase after a house. We now have had to undergo four rounds of downsizing and salary cuts and have been forced to infuse a bit more capital into the company. The good news is that, like Assured Guaranty in monolines, IAC will be among the few entities left standing when the industry turns around. IAC, like most of our portfolio companies, is relatively unleveraged—because we believe that high levels of debt are inappropriate for companies that are highly cyclical and have commodity price risks to boot. Once it became clear that GM and Chrysler needed federal bailouts, we joined with both of them, the unions, and other suppliers to lobby for federal guaranty of the money owed to suppliers by GM and Chrysler; for other federally assisted restructuring of the two companies; and for the cash for clunkers program to encourage people to scrap old cars and buy new ones. This is green in both the environmental sense and in terms of the economy. With or without that program, IAC has been gaining market share, with $300 million of current business having been transferred to it in the past 90 days from failed or failing competitors. While this is not nearly enough to make up for the huge drop in unit production, it does convince us that IAC will be fine when volume returns to a more normal level of 13 to 14 million cars per year in the United States. Our country scraps between 12.5 and 13 million cars annually and there is also population growth, so unless there are fewer and fewer cars per capita, the annual average sales must be in the range of 13 to 14 million, versus the 9 million or so that will be sold this year. We also acquired in Europe Stankiewicz a high quality € 150 million producer of automotive acoustical products. This will enhance our market share in that segment and bring us additional technology.

We now are moving more aggressively to commit our portfolio, although I must admit, most importantly and most surprisingly, to the new government-assisted programs. In the fall of 2008, when Treasury Secretary Paulson correctly announced a program to buy from the banks the kinds of toxic assets that slew AIG, Bear Stearns, Citibank, Lehman Brothers, Merrill Lynch, and the Reserve Fund, the Bush administration changed its emphasis to direct investment in hundreds of banks. I continue to believe that neither the financial system nor the housing market will straighten out until there is a clearing event for the toxic assets. The Troubled Asset Relief Program (TARP) is a good way to fill the holes, but just pumping in more TARP money is treating the symptoms rather than curing the disease. Banks will not lend with normal aggressiveness until and unless they believe that their existing portfolio will not blow up even worse. The only way to give them that confidence will be the public-private investment portfolio (PPIP) proposed by Treasury Secretary Geithner, coupled with the additional TARP money needed to replace the loss on the sale of toxic assets. We are seeking to be big players in the PPIP, just as we were in the Term Asset-Backed Securities Loan Facility (TALF).* We closed in September 2009 on close to a $1 billion in Public-Private Investment Funds (PPIFs), which were created under the Legacy Securities Public-Private Investment Program (PPIP). Invesco is among the firms the government has selected to help get toxic assets off the balance sheets of troubled banks. Our equity will be matched 50/50 by TARP money.

TALF has reopened the asset-backed commercial paper (ABCP) market, and if applied with aggressive encouragement of the banks to sell, PPIP will reopen the longer-term securitization market big time. That is what we need to get the economy going again, especially now that commercial real estate loans, in general, and commercial mortgage-backed securitizations, in particular, are about to blow up, with $750 billion due through 2011 and $1.5 trillion due through 2013.

In the first TALF auction, we were a major buyer of Ford Motor Credit ABCP. The yield on it was 6.05 percent, and the government guaranteed a non-recourse loan for 90 percent of the purchase price at 2.70 percent. The yield on the equity sliver was about 35 percent. Auto ABCP had been essentially unsalable for many months, so this made funding available, albeit at a high price. Each subsequent auction developed increasingly lower asset yields, so we did not buy any. In fact, in the fourth auction, we had American Home

---

* *Author's note:* Term Asset-Backed Securities Loan Facility (TALF) was created by the Federal Reserve to add liquidity back into the credit markets by meeting the credit needs of small business and consumers. The Fed would issue them asset backed securities (ABS).

Mortgage issue $600 million at about 3 percent to cut its costs of financing advance.

In September 2009, I had to make another trip back to Singapore and I dreaded the idea that I would get another urgent phone call about another major institution failing. If that was the case, I would be banned from Singapore forever. Thankfully, I was welcomed back to Singapore without another crisis.

Epilogue

Since this book went to print in late fall of 2009, the lack of liquidity was still impacting business, as well as the housing market, and economists and market strategists were debating on whether we were in a "W" or "U" shaped recovery. The fear is out there, but as you have read in all of my contacts' stories, fear is not stopping them from thriving. In fact, fear is actually driving them to challenge themselves, innovate, to think outside the box, and look for opportunities where many would just see carnage.

Whether acquiring an investment boutique like Peter Cohen, to transform and expand his business in what he calls "going back to the future," or planning years ahead for a disaster and streamlining a business like Mike Jackson, or by blazing a new trail and buying a "sick bank" like Wilbur Ross and Richard LeFrak—good businesses thrive by thinking outside the box. The strategies highlighted in this book all have one common thread—these individuals have criteria they stick to, they believe in their guts, and they are not afraid to make decisions some in the public may doubt.

Innovation is one of the greatest tools of capitalism. Jerry Greenwald's words on thriving are dead on: ". . . you can't save your way out of a crisis. You cannot cut your costs enough to become successful." Thriving in this new economy means not to be blinded by a moment in a crisis. It means to seize that moment, embrace it, and turn it into a moment of opportunity.

AFTERWORD

Mayor Rudy Giuliani

When I was a kid growing up in Dodgers-mad Brooklyn, I liked to wear my Yankees uniform. I suspected it would get me into trouble—and it certainly did—but there was something appealing about doing the opposite of what everyone expects. Taking chances often leads to enormous opportunities, both in life and as an investor in our current crisis.

I have worked with Lori Ann LaRocco at CNBC's *Squawk Box,* and I've been impressed with her ear for interesting, useful information for the investor. Her book is full of insight and also reflects a contrarian, daring viewpoint that can lead to exciting prospects.

In 2009, the financial landscape is daunting, and many financial experts have conflicting advice for the investor. American workers are being laid off at a dizzying pace, and our nation is indebted to China for a sum approaching $1 trillion. Whatever we think about the current administration's response to the financial crisis, we have to remember that the stock market rises and falls based not just on their decision, but on the judgments of millions of individual investors. Each investor has a chance to look for openings and ways to thrive even in the bleakest landscape.

When I first took office in 1994, New York City faced very serious challenges. New Yorkers saw mountains of trash on the streets, panhandlers accosted visitors, the murder rate was out of control, and sky-high taxes were chasing the city's business base out of town. A miserable bond rating reflected all of these concerns and made borrowing that much more expensive.

My team became contrarians. We decided to believe in a New York City that didn't exist yet. We embraced a vision that called for change many thought impossible, in a city that had long been deemed "ungovernable." By the time I left office, there were no squeegee men, trash was under control, crime rates had plummeted, and our bond rating had soared to a 30-year high. We had overcome terrible obstacles through will and a stubborn belief in what New York City could and should be.

Today's investors need to imagine what the American economy can and will look like, rather than reacting solely to today's reality. Many of the business legends interviewed here share that perspective and Lori Ann LaRocco shares their insights and adds to them. Our market will be powerful again if we continue to appreciate how it built our country and how we will build it again.

Rudolph W. Giuliani is the chairman and CEO of the security consulting business Giuliani Partners, LLC, which he founded in January 2002. He was the mayor of New York City from 1994 to 2001.

When Giuliani first took office, poverty was something many New Yorkers knew, with one out of every seven New Yorkers collecting welfare. By implementing what many refer to as the largest and most successful welfare-to-work initiative in the nation, Giuliani cut welfare rolls in half, while helping get 640,000 individuals off government assistance. Tax cuts were also a central part of his economic agenda, with a record of over $2.5 billion in tax reductions, including the personal income tax, commercial rent tax, sales tax on clothing for purchases up to $110, and the hotel occupancy tax. These reforms transformed the $2.3 billion budget deficit Giuliani inherited into a multibillion dollar surplus. In addition to his economic accomplishments, Giuliani is most known for his leadership during the 9/11 terrorist attacks, when he garnered international attention and was called "America's Mayor."

ACKNOWLEDGMENTS

I would like to take this time to thank those who were instrumental in my accomplishment in writing *Thriving in the New Economy*. Thank you, Richard, for encouraging me to write a book. You planted the seeds months ago, and it got me thinking of undertaking such a project. I also want to thank Don for suggesting Wiley. It has been an amazing experience. I have loved every minute working with Shannon, Beth, and Kate. Thank you!

I also want to say thank you to all my contacts who participated in this book and shared their stories. They were thought provoking and inspirational. And finally, I would like to say thank you to Mark Hoffman, president of CNBC, for giving me the green light to write this book.

About The Author

Lori Ann LaRocco is the senior talent producer at CNBC and has the ear of some of the world's biggest business minds. Lori Ann has been working at the network since 2000. She was first hired as one of Maria Bartiromo's producers on her evening show, *Market Week.* Lori Ann produced and booked interviews with some of the biggest and previously unattainable names in business. In 2005, Lori Ann was tapped to help with the relaunch of CNBC's flagship morning show, *Squawk Box.*

Lori Ann's track record has garnered trust and respect from Wall Street rainmakers and Washington leaders and insiders, who confide in Lori Ann first with their breaking billion dollar business deals and policy announcements. Lori Ann continues to add to her roster of contacts, as well as field produce million dollar shows like *Squawk Box Across America* at Gillette Stadium. Prior to CNBC, Lori Ann worked as an anchor, reporter, and assignment editor in local news around the country for seven years. Lori Ann is also a proud and busy hockey, baseball, soccer, karate, and dance mom of three children.

INDEX